HOME STILLS

BASTIENNE SCHMIDT

to Nicole and
Myla!!
Lot's of love!
xo Bastienne

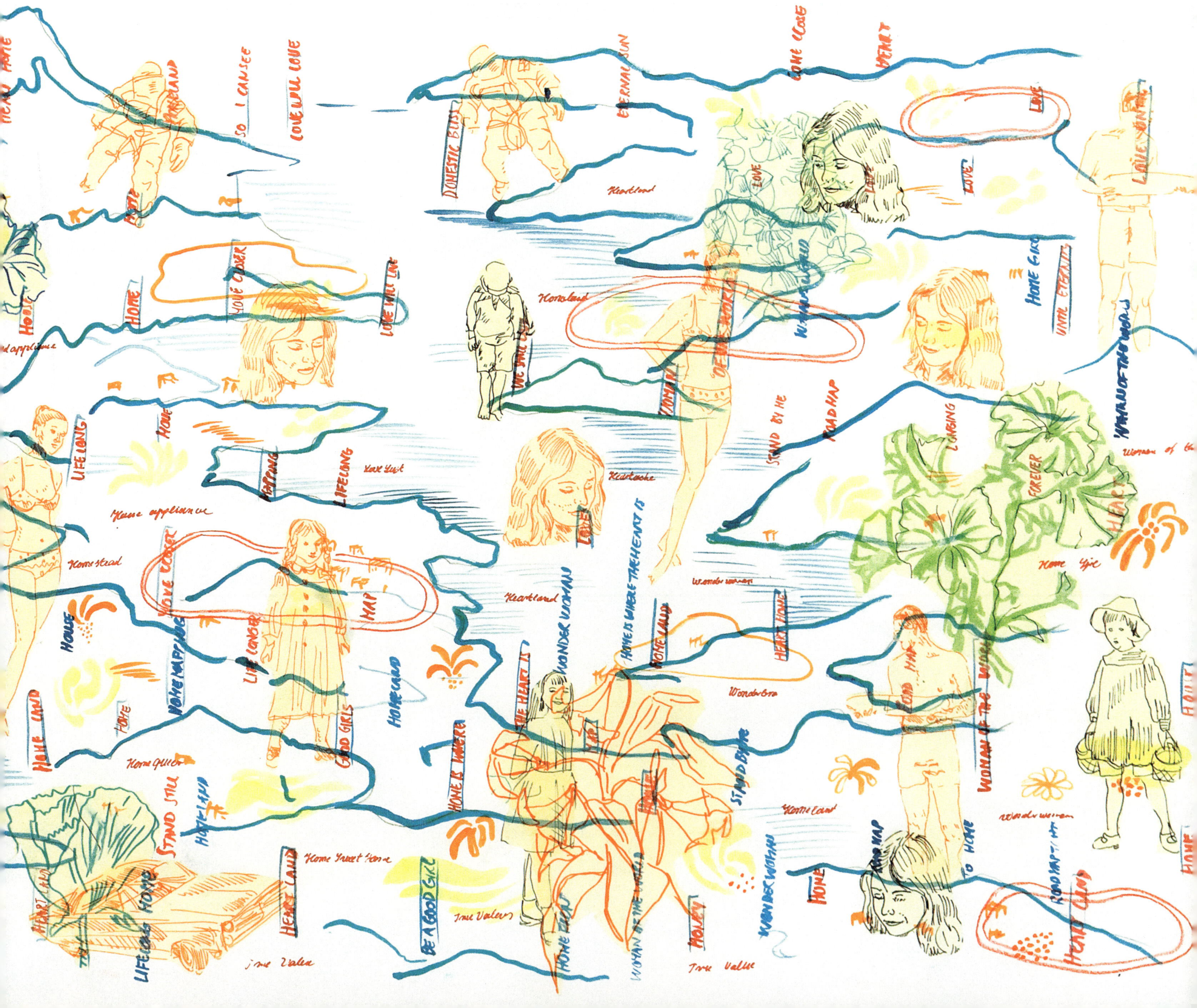

HOME STILLS

BASTIENNE SCHMIDT

jovis

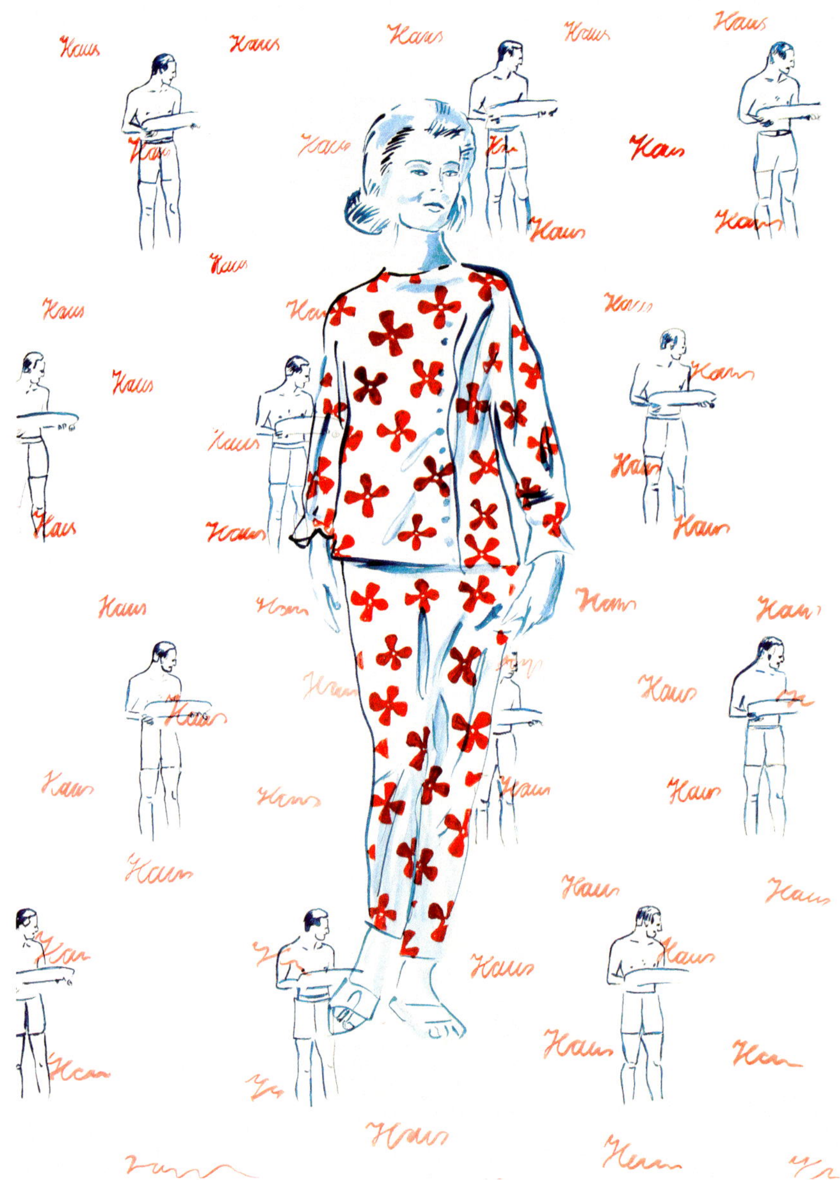

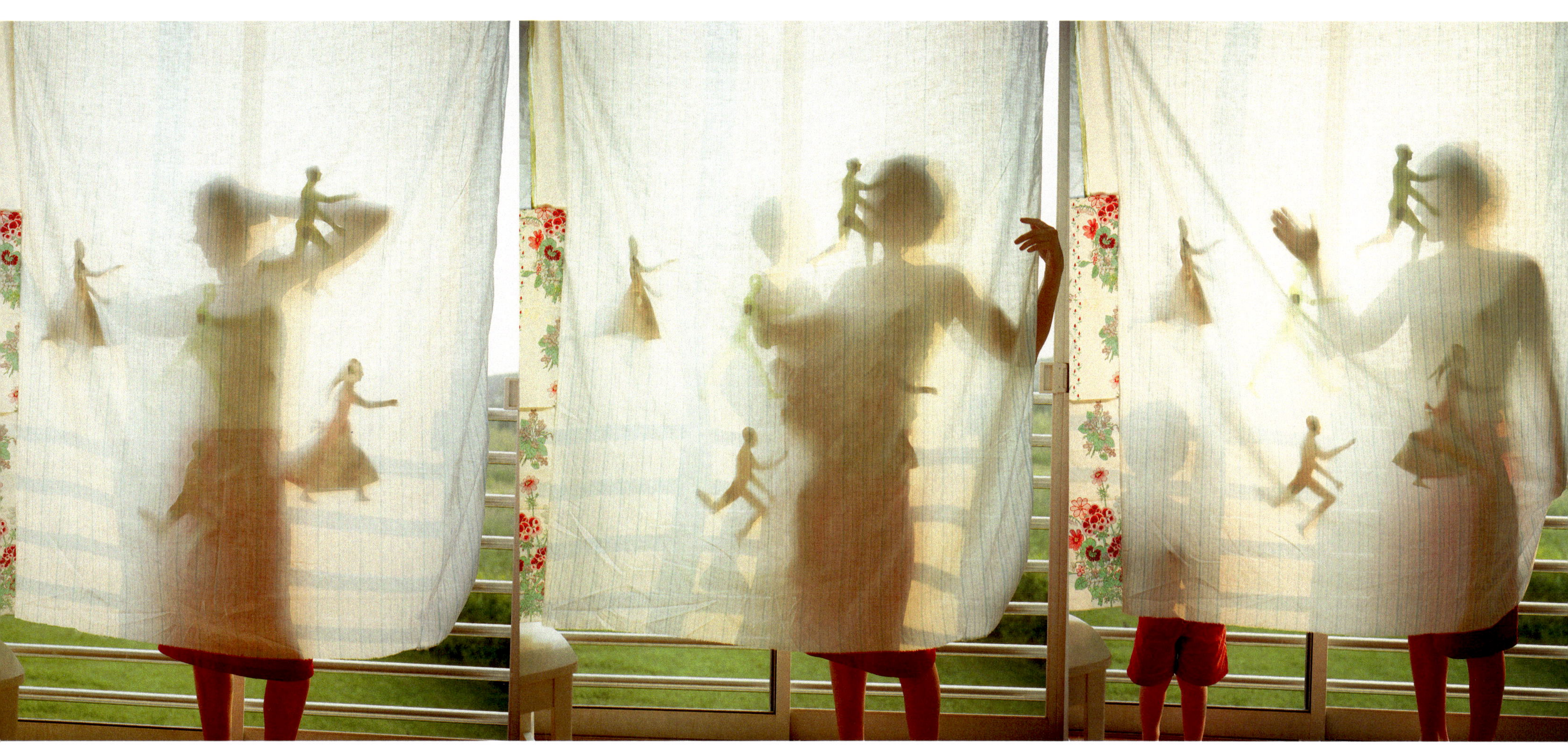

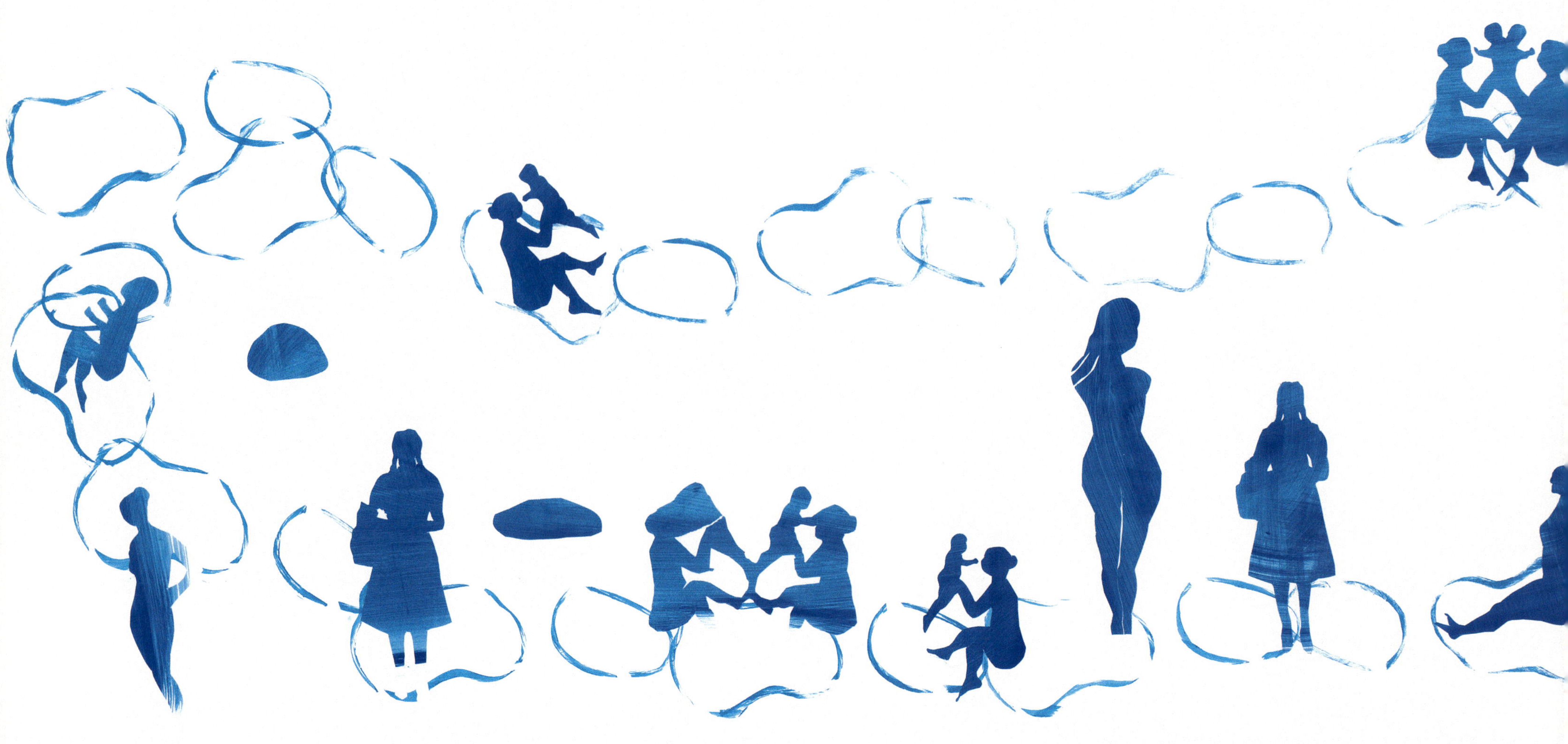

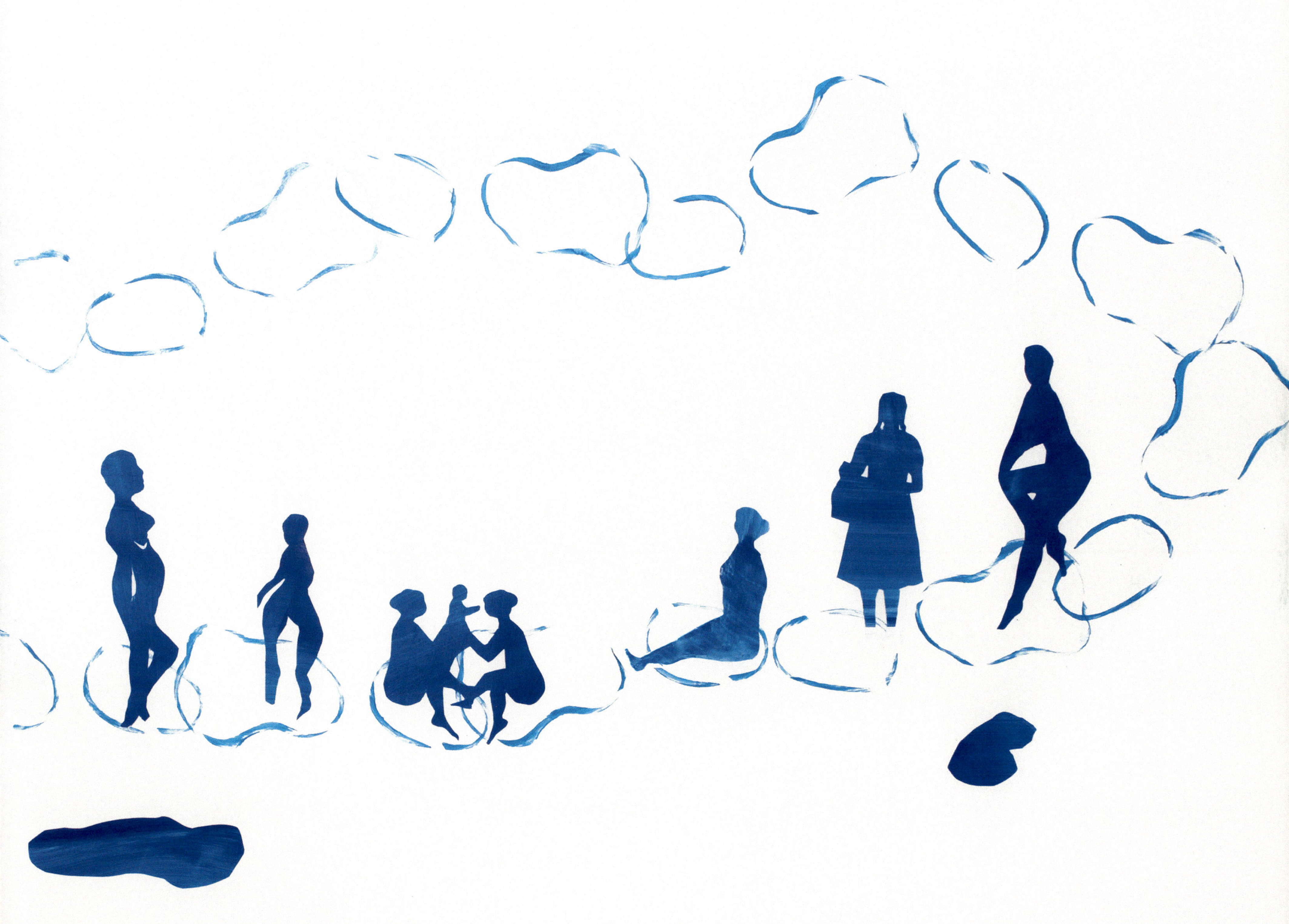

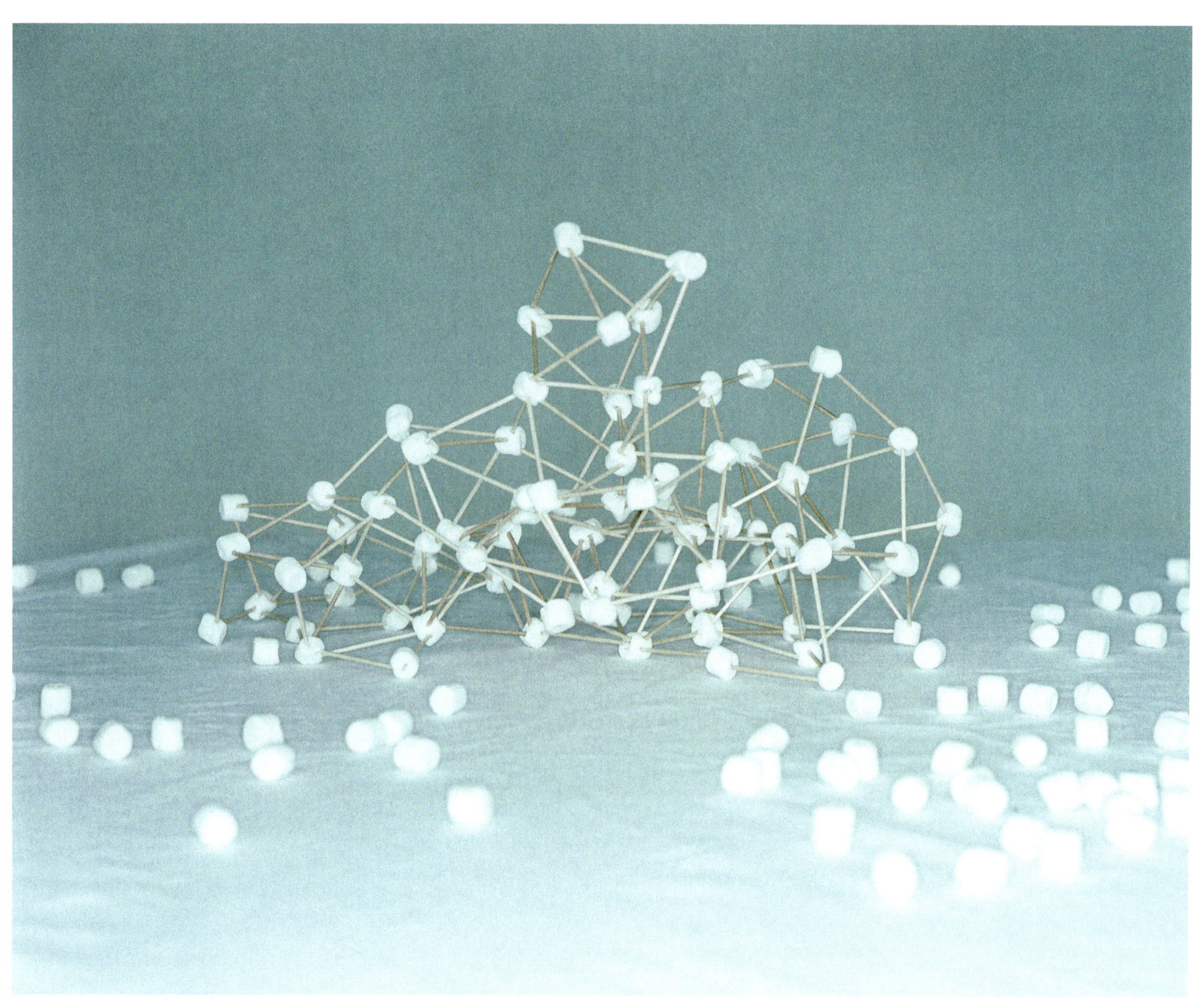

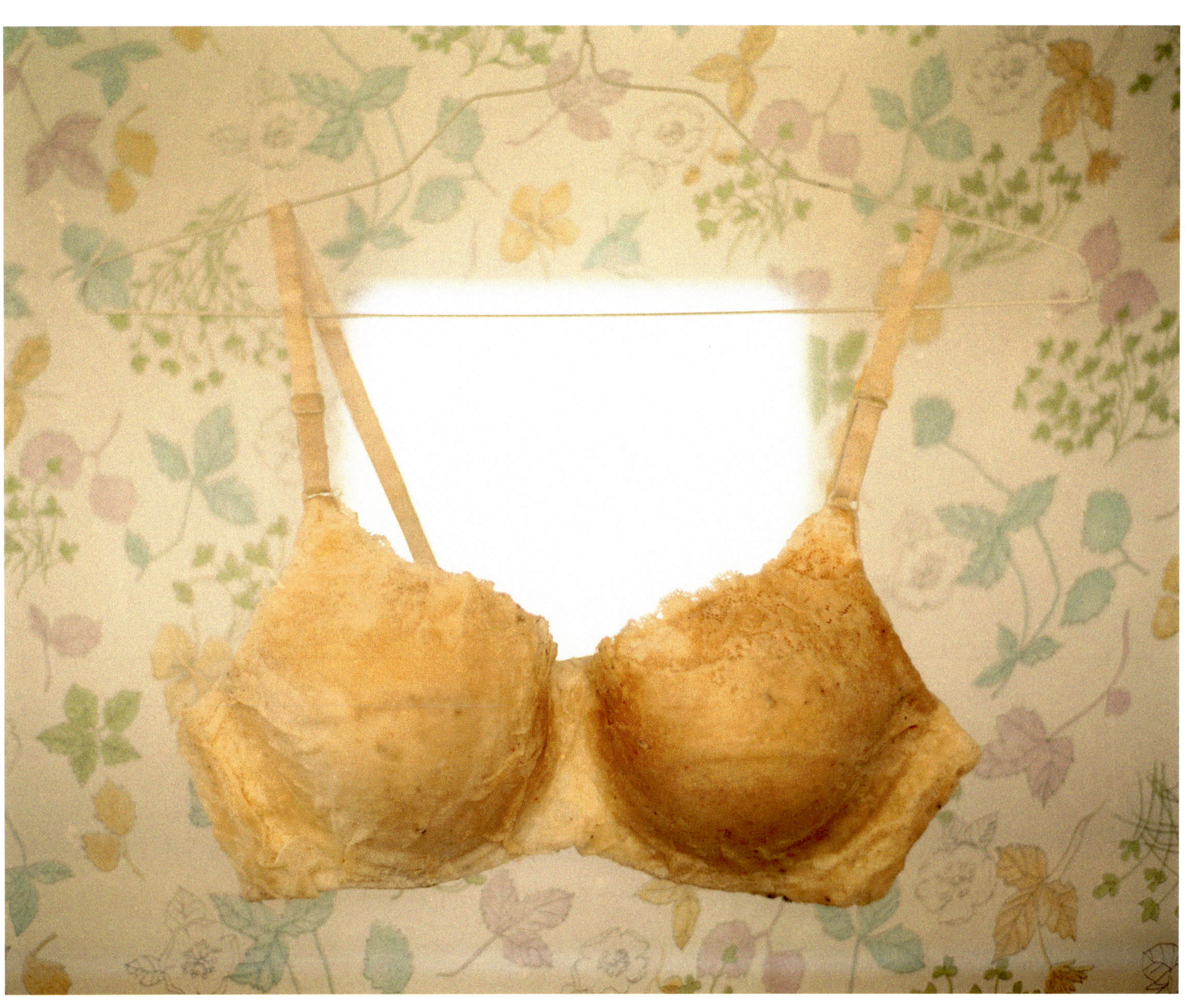

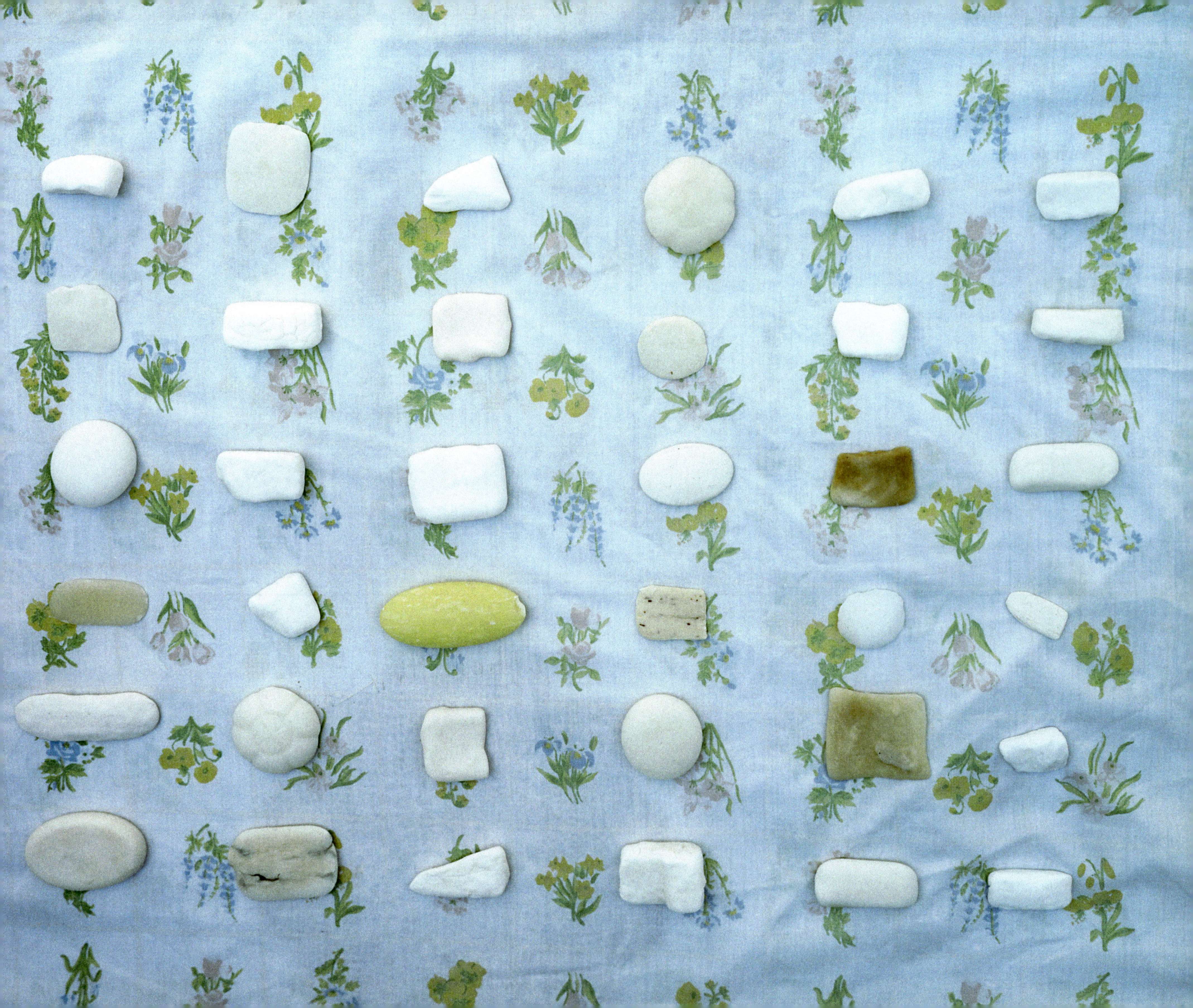

A WOMAN'S PLACE

Vicki Goldberg

Home Stills leave home or stick around. Bastienne Schmidt wanders, metaphorically or on foot, in and out of a woman's life and imagination—her own and by inference many others. At home and not-home, amid order and disorder, roaming and staying put, hiding out in plain sight, she builds narratives where multiple meanings glimmer below the surface and ambiguities fill the frame. "The Blue Cycle" proposes the circle of (woman's) life with drawings of a child, a young girl who might be Dorothy in Oz, a man or two but more female types: sexpot, sophisticate, mothers with babies. The photographs expand the circle into concentric realms.

Photographers have an advantage. They can rearrange life for a moment or two. They can make visible what's on their minds while the rest of us are stuck inside our heads. Schmidt's photographs refashion the world that life's cycle has already remade for her. She stages images of a woman (the photographer, for she is her own model) at home, with children, as well as inside other people's homes and imagined lives. She wanders away from home for a day in search of the freedom to leave home for anywhere, at anytime, which came with an earlier part of the cycle when she was single.

Once children came into Schmidt's life, another world did too: tiny toys that lived miniature lives. They beckoned her to imagine "an artistic reorganization, in the midst of the chaos of a household"[1] (while most of us were merely imagining the toys being miraculously put away). In her photographs, minuscule knights and warriors cascade down from on high behind a curtain and pint-size adults run purposefully across other curtains, defying reason in favor of artistic reorganization.

Disorganization makes itself at home. "Tax Time" has spewed papers over everything. In "Money Counter," coins sit on a table, some in neat little stacks, others waiting for order. Life's nagging repetitions discreetly present themselves: the floor needs to be vacuumed again, pieces of paper must be picked up. What's really at work is entropy, the relentless decline of everything into disorder. In one engaging and distinctly feminine riff on the grid, that staple of modern art, Schmidt has imposed regularity on half-used soap: mathematically correct lines across a flower-patterned fabric. (Sol Lewitt would not approve.) The soaps have become muddled shapes in the service of cleanliness; regular or not, they are on the way to their own kind of death and disappearance because we are trying so hard to avoid exactly that.

Where Cindy Sherman has imagined herself as someone else—anyone, everyone—Bastienne Schmidt imagines herself in other places. She inserts herself into places where she does not live, attempting to think herself into other lives. She tries on what it might feel like inside a mac-and-cheese residence, a cheap motel, or a place where you dress up and put on house slippers to sit in a row of oversize, tacky armchairs. She tries out a grand Long Island mansion or two with vistas of still waters. For a thirtieth of a second, she inhabits another life, as if she were a subdued version of Woody Allen's Zelig. Only artists, actors, a few people on reality TV swapping-lives shows—and a photographer—get to act out the sense of being inside someone else's life, though envy or compassion can stir that sense in anyone.

Schmidt wanders a lot in *Home Stills*, across her home territory, the fields and woods on the eastern end of Long Island. Years ago, when still a fairly recent immigrant, she wandered around the country with a camera in her hand in search of America, a search that produced a book called *American Dreams*.[2] Once she had a family and much less time, wandering without a fixed goal along the road to unexpected discovery turned in her mind "from a necessity into a luxury." Her "roaming" photographs minimally reconstruct a period of her life and comment on the kind of on-the-road photography that has produced books like Len Jenshel's *Travels in the American West*, Alec Soth's *Sleeping by the Mississippi*, Burk Uzzle's *Just Add Water,* and Schmidt's own.

She thinks of herself in her *wanderbilder* as a lone housewife in the unlikely act of walking out of the picture into the proverbial sunset; a journey commonly reserved for cowboys in westerns. Her territory is too domesticated and suburban to fit the allusion: once she walks along the yellow do-not-pass lines of a tree-lined street, a middle-of-the-road path quite unlike the lonesome, flatland highways that Dorothea Lange and Robert Frank photographed. It must have crossed the mind of many a mother, faced with caterwauls and runny noses, dust balls and yet another dinner to provide, that it might be a relief to step out of the picture. The housewife and mother's need to be alone isn't a wild west restlessness but a temporary desire for respite, hardly the cowboy's solitary drive to write his own road movie by inventing his own road under his horse's hooves. A few women do up and abandon their children, a baffling notion for most of us, but in general women who leave have either been abused or fallen prey to passion. For the rest, there are pictures in the mind, which a photographer can transfer to paper.

Schmidt's photographs are composed of light, color, geometry, and secrets. Light is the soul of the medium; the word *photography* means "light writing." Schmidt creates geometries of light as that elusive, formless element responds to the rectilinear rules we have laid down for our right-angle homes. In *Home Stills,* rectangles of light blaze in doors and windows, strict shapes of light hover on walls and floors. In one picture, windows cast three light squares across three solid rectangles (a mirror, two pictures) that hang on the wall, as if the squares in a painting by Joseph Albers had decided to get up and dance. And in the darkness just before night definitively clamps down on earth, a black house at an odd tilt has four small squares of light cut out of it like features in a jack-o-lantern. Light can subvert geometry as well: looking down a staircase in a house that is probably white but registers as gray in the photograph, the camera angle skews the perspective while sunlight throws blurred reflections and clouds like splotches of paint across the walls, turning a rational interior into a Frank Gehry experience.

Schmidt's color can be as punchy as an exclamation mark: the normative yellow staircase in that irregular white house, a bright red dress atop a haphazard mass of gray cut logs, and most striking of all, Schmidt's red skirt and stockings above her green shadow. (Uncommon as it is to take a picture of one's own standing feet, this photograph commemorates an uncommon occasion, the day that Bastienne Schmidt became an American citizen.) Other times, other palettes: a room may turn monochrome, like the white room with a white bed covered with white pieces of paper, the room with turquoise walls that impose a turquoise aura on everything, the green glaze coating a hallway and glancing over a figure's clothing.

And then there are the secrets, first and foremost the photographer herself, hiding in full view. Though there is a thread of autobiography here, the protagonist remains essentially unseen, faceless, unidentifiable. She turns her back to us. Typically a viewer is expected to identify with a person seen from the back, as both look in the same direction. Here, though the experience is shared, the back becomes a denial: you shall not know me intimately, I will only let you into my ideas. She hides behind and blurs behind sheer curtains, behind a screen, behind a complicated, spider-web like pattern of threads, behind her *hair*. Light obscures her as surely as darkness does, and sometimes only a shadow describes her. The story in *Home Stills*, about a woman imagining other homes and an earlier life with its freedoms, is a story that extends to many women's lives. Maintaining a private face, a kind of physical anonymity in the cause of widening the reference, is nonetheless an anomaly in an era when millions of faces (and bodies) are unveiled on the Web every day and ordinary folk scramble to achieve their fifteen minutes of fame in one visual medium or another. Schmidt is not just protecting her privacy but saying that women even today are not fully visible but seen through a mesh of perceptions. She presents images from cinema, too—women portraying women in a medium that projects popular notions of women's roles in society—but renders them hazy behind diaphanous flowered fabrics. This is not an entirely outmoded notion, much as we'd like to think so. The preliminary report of the Global Media Monitoring Project in 2010 found that only 24 percent of people seen, heard, or read about in the news worldwide are female, only 16 percent of news stories focus specifically on women, and fewer than one out of five experts interviewed is female. In effect, the news presents a world in which women are largely absent—or invisible.[3]

Not exactly secret, nor always readily apparent, are multiple layers of meaning. Photography has an uncanny ability: a single photograph can encompass almost as many types of expression within its borders as a library does—fiction and non-fiction, short story and document, history, sociology, theater, history of art, fantasy, myth, poetry. Every photograph that hasn't yet met Photoshop, as well as most that are not pure abstraction, qualify as both fact and fiction. Whatever is in the picture is a fact of sorts—it was there, in front of the lens, and looked very like that at one particular angle and in a particular light. But photographs are now acknowledged as fiction more readily than fact: excerpts—the eyes would have seen more than the viewfinder did—and obviously not the real thing but a representation and version of reality, however that is to be defined in these doubting days.

Schmidt's *Home Stills* are almost as variously informed and informative as a card catalogue. Take "Laundry Spiral," a picture of a woman standing in the center of a spiral made of rolled-up laundry, her child running toward her across the lawn. Non-fiction, yes; the woman, the child, the lawn, the autumn tree, and the spiral were all where the photograph says they were. Fiction, yes, or theater: constructed, staged, and invented. Autobiography too: her son, her lawn, her tree, her environment. And her laundry. Married women, mothers, women living with male partners generally do more of the household laundry than men do (even today), so add to the other elements a statement about women. She looks trapped in the middle of that spiral, as if the dirty or unfolded clothes had her in their grip. (I remember that when my children were very young it occurred to me that I might be suffocated by the weight, the sheer quantity, and the fierce repetitiveness of the wash.)

Then there's mythology or symbolism: the spiral is frequently said to represent the Goddess, the womb, femaleness, fertility, female sexuality—and/or the evolution of the universe. On top of that, the photograph explicitly points to art history: Robert Smithson's "Spiral Jetty," which in its subdued, stony palette is almost as multicolored as Schmidt's conglomerated shirts and trousers. She says she chose soft materials because women artists often use them: another statement about women. It's possible to infer in addition a subtle psychological conundrum: her child runs toward her, and she begins to raise her arms as if prepared to receive and embrace him, but if she is indeed trapped in her own female nature, can he trespass on the spiral or negotiate it? The photograph very quietly hints at the difficulties of motherhood.

Or take "Woman in Field with Water Tower," which refers to Andrew Wyeth's *Christina's World*, the famous painting of a young paralyzed woman in a brown field crawling toward a house on the horizon. Art history again: Schmidt freely borrows ideas or images from painting, photography and film, a practice entirely appropriate to an era of appropriation and a time when the media have put the history of all manner of imagery before our eyes. "Woman in Field with Water Tower" rings a number of changes on Wyeth; Schmidt always reworks the sources of her inspirations. We know the woman in question is not paralyzed. What stands on the horizon is not a house, not a home, but a water tower—one with a particularly efficient shape that always strikes me as a vague sort of female symbol. The woman not only does not lean hungrily toward the tower as Christina does toward the house but walks in another direction, and the dry stalks on the left lean away as well.

"Woman on Red Daybed" makes an even more obvious reference to

Edward Hopper's *A Woman in the Sun*. The changes are many—light room vs. dark, clothed vs. nude, sitting vs. standing, facing left vs. right—but the respectful nod to the Hopper is unmistakable. The stillness, the air of contemplation, and the power of light are more than close enough. Hopper's influence on art has been immense, on artists as disparate as Eric Fischl and Red Grooms, as well as myriad photographers from Harry Callahan and Robert Frank to Robert Adams and Stephen Shore. A recent and much more exact rendition of *A Woman in the Sun* was exhibited at the 2010 Whitney Biennial: R. H. Quayman's *Distracting Distance, Chapter 16*, an installation with a monochrome image of a nude woman standing in the light by an image of one of the Whitney Museum's distinctive windows.

Several photographs of Schmidt, a.k.a the woman, looking out of a window reprise a theme that was common in nineteenth century painting (and occasionally appeared in the twentieth; see Salvador Dali's *Woman at the Window*). This subject had a lot to do with the way women were regarded in the past, as domestic creatures that did not belong outside but may have longed for something beyond the hearth. More than two thousand years ago, Euripides wrote, "A woman should be good for everything at home, but abroad good for nothing," a sentiment that reverberated across centuries. Schmidt's photographs pick up on the history of women's roles and how they were seen; commentary informed by both art history and sociology.

At the same time they can be seen as metaphors for photography itself. Looking, looking—what else would a photographer do? (Coincidentally, the first known photograph is an 1826 view out of a window by Nicéphore Niépce.) From the beach, Schmidt looks out to sea, a subject practically owned by Caspar David Friedrich in the nineteenth century. From the corner of a house, Schmidt looks out at a field. What is beyond our constricted personal compass, or beyond even our vision of our little lives? Earth-bound photography does not, cannot answer, nor can painting (which tries hard); a camera can only pose the question and picture the wish to venture farther than the place where our feet are planted.

Schmidt's extensive catalogue of implied genres includes mysteries aplenty. In "The Turquoise Room," she hides behind mosquito netting, her child is practically deconstructed by movement on film, and the very pictures on the wall are carefully wrapped and entirely covered from view. Whatever goes on here, and why? And what is Schmidt doing in the picture where she is dressed in red on a heap of sawn-up logs? She can scarcely be wandering across this hassle of wood. Her large, bright figure rising into the sky and her widespread legs declare her dominance, yet she has no arms: a conqueror without adequate means.

The narratives these photographs propose are open-ended, even open-sided, half a story without a perceptible closing half. They raise questions they do not deign to answer. If the scenes that go beyond a mere snippet of autobiography into the region of ideas sprang from her imagination, they ask to enter ours. We may fill in the blanks ourselves or accept these as stories that end with a comma rather than a period. Yet one cannot miss the sense that a woman is mostly seen through a screen [of preconceptions] that clouds her image; she is unmistakably there but not often fully present. Working on the edge of ambiguity, Bastienne Schmidt can drive a point home still.

1 Quotes are either from notes that Schmidt herself made or from interviews with VG in May 2010.

2 Full disclosure: I wrote the introduction to this 1997 book published by Stemmle.

3 http://www.africafiles.org/article.asp?ID=23064
The information is from a preliminary report, based on a sample of forty-two countries in Africa, Asia, Latin America, the Caribbean, Pacific Islands, and Europe. Retrieved May 20, 2010.

HOME STILLS

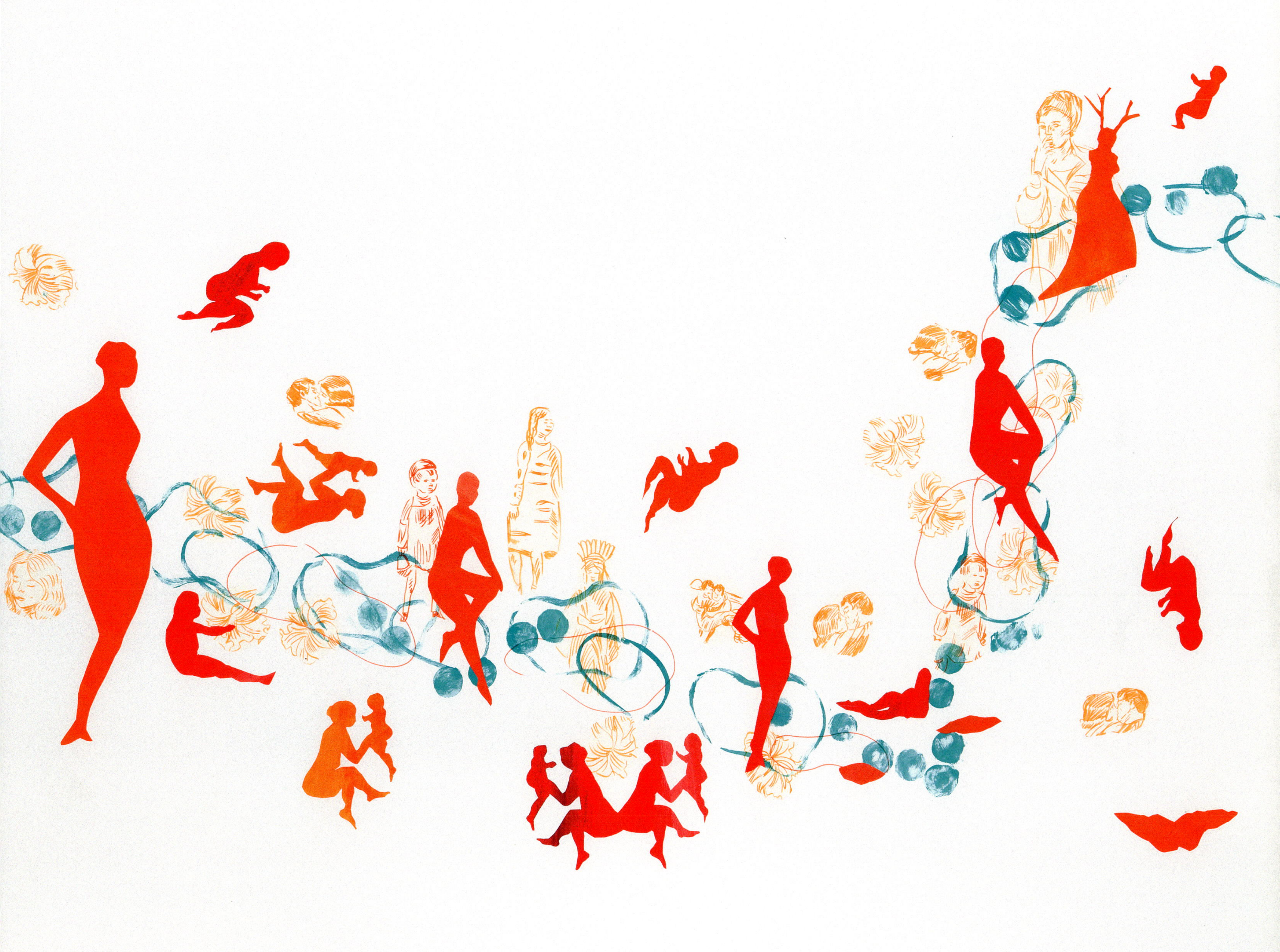

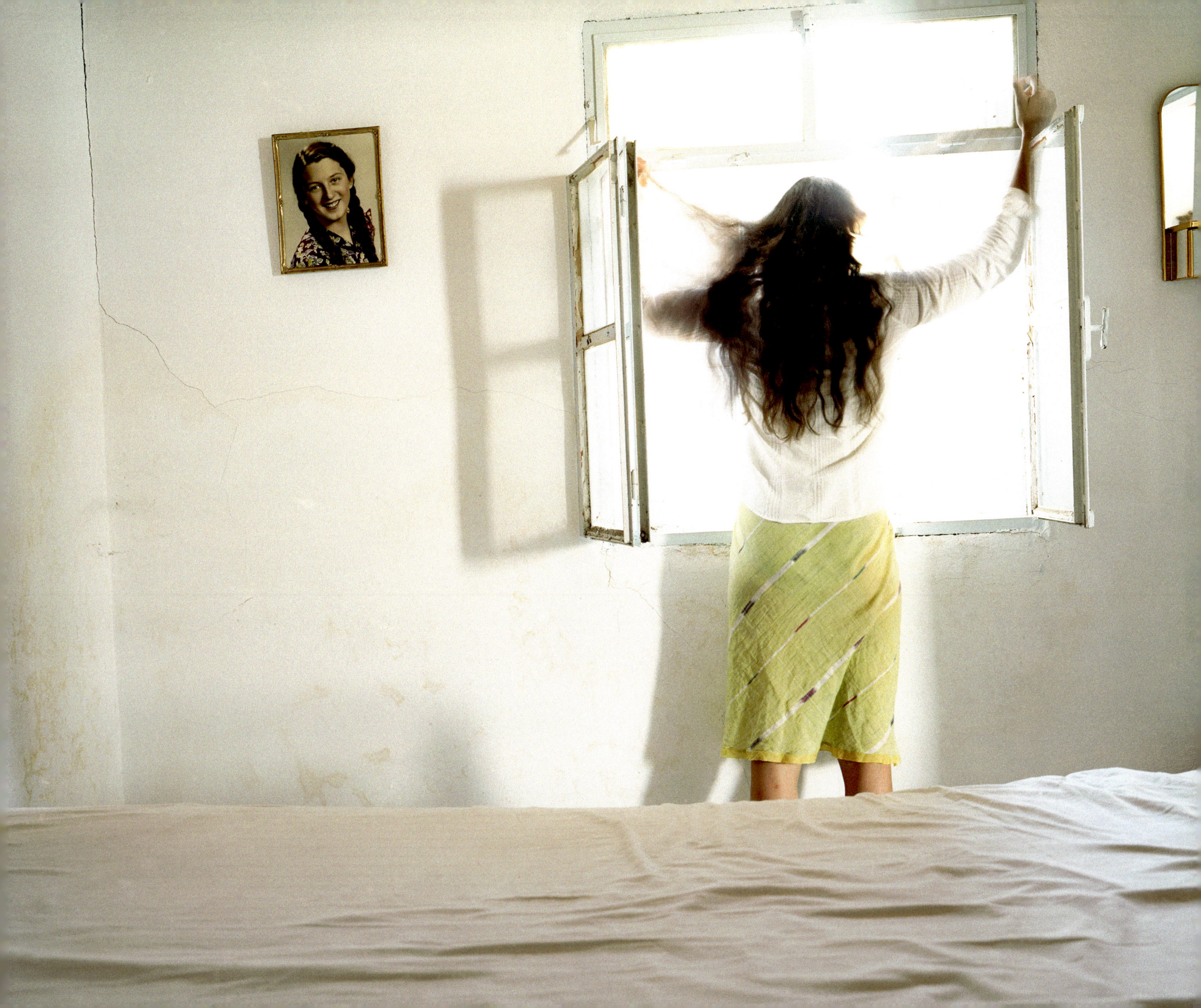

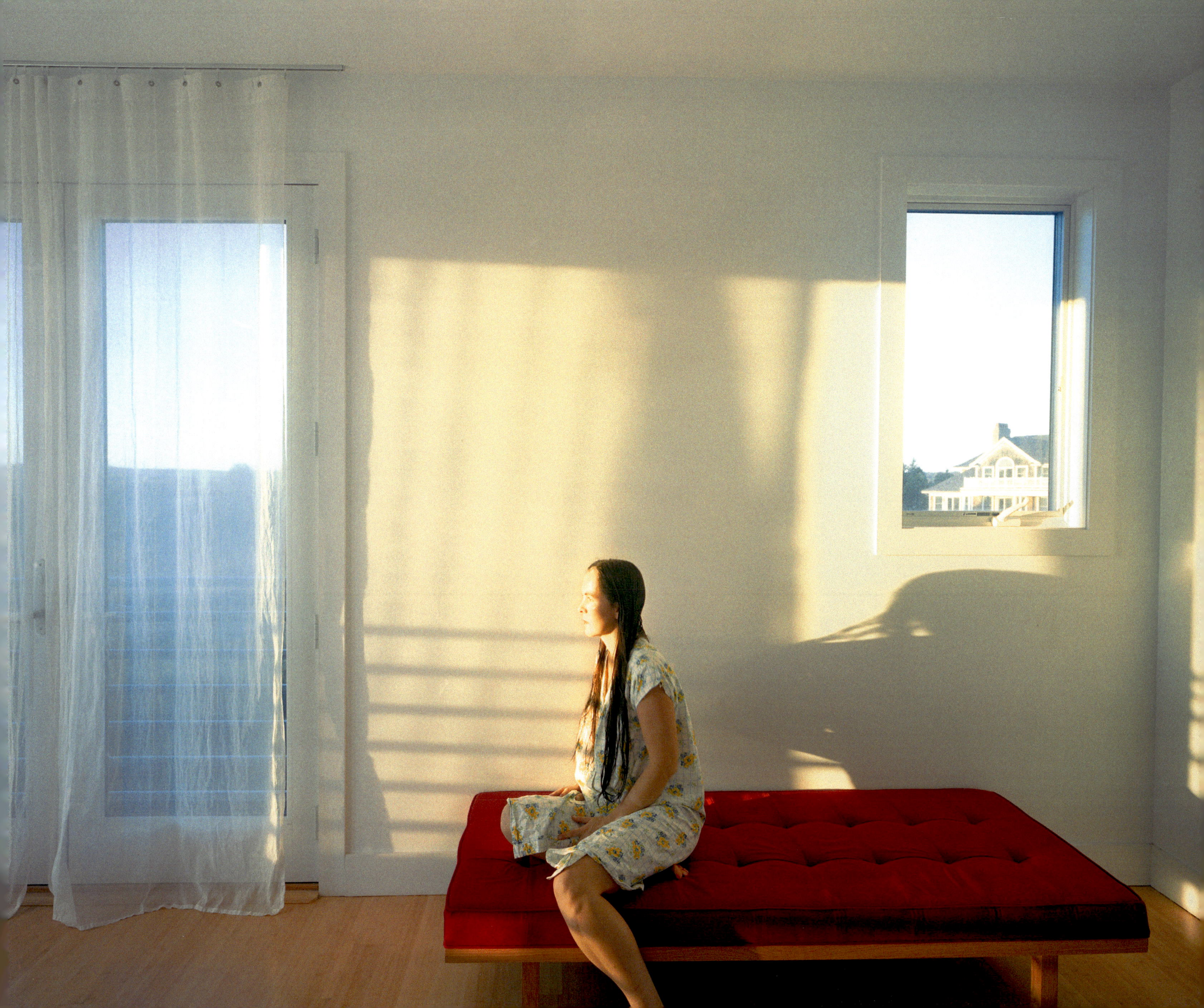

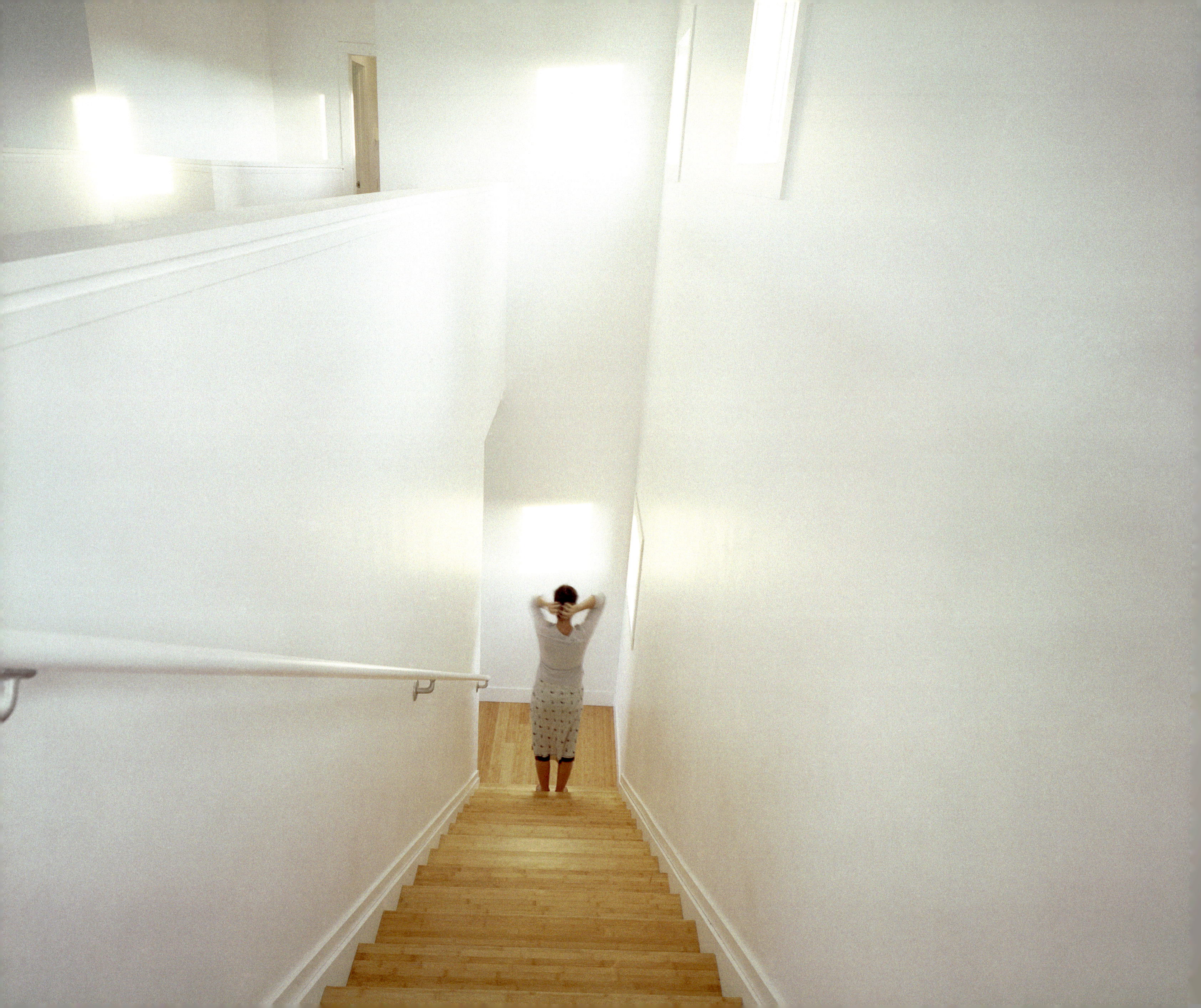

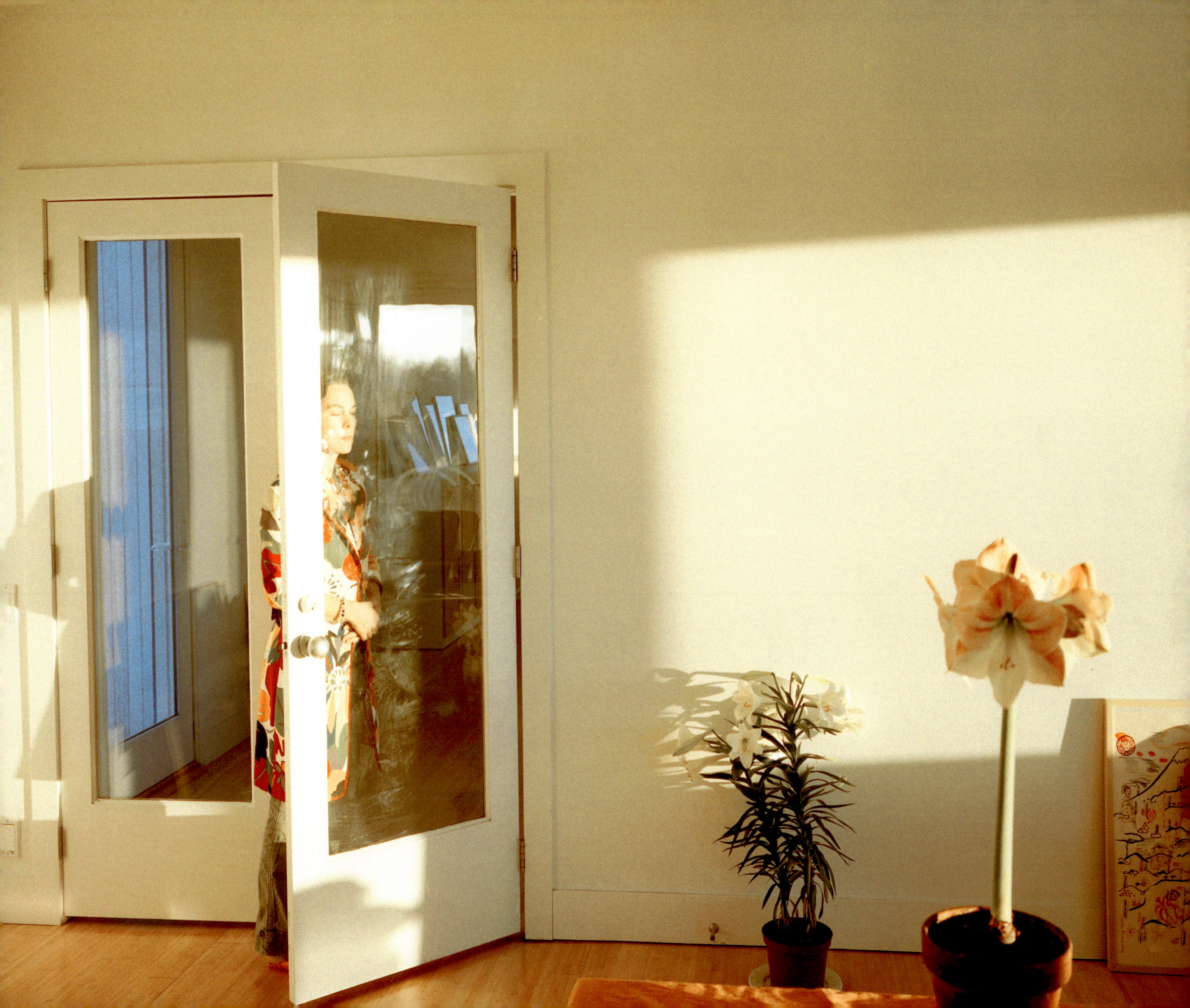

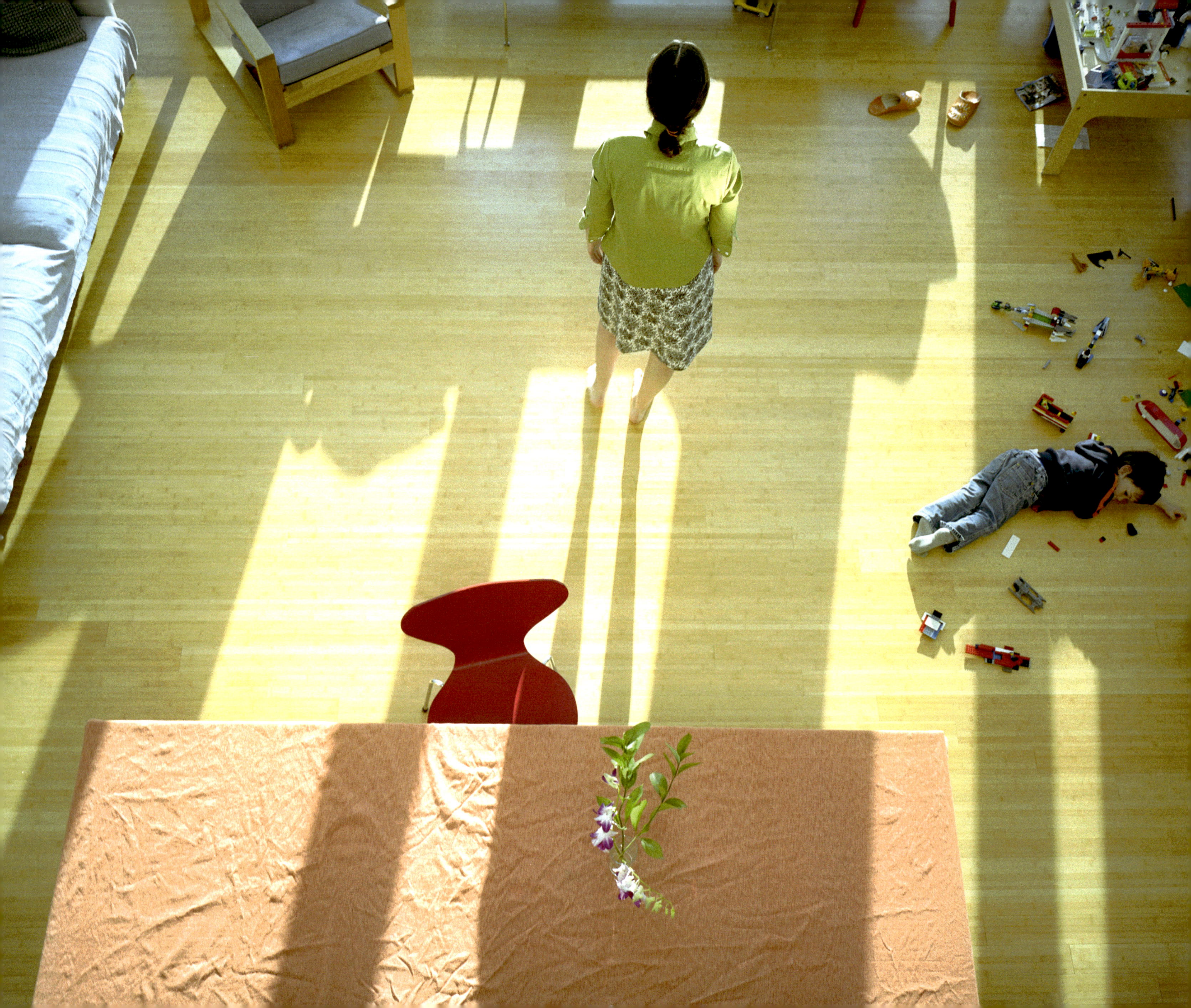

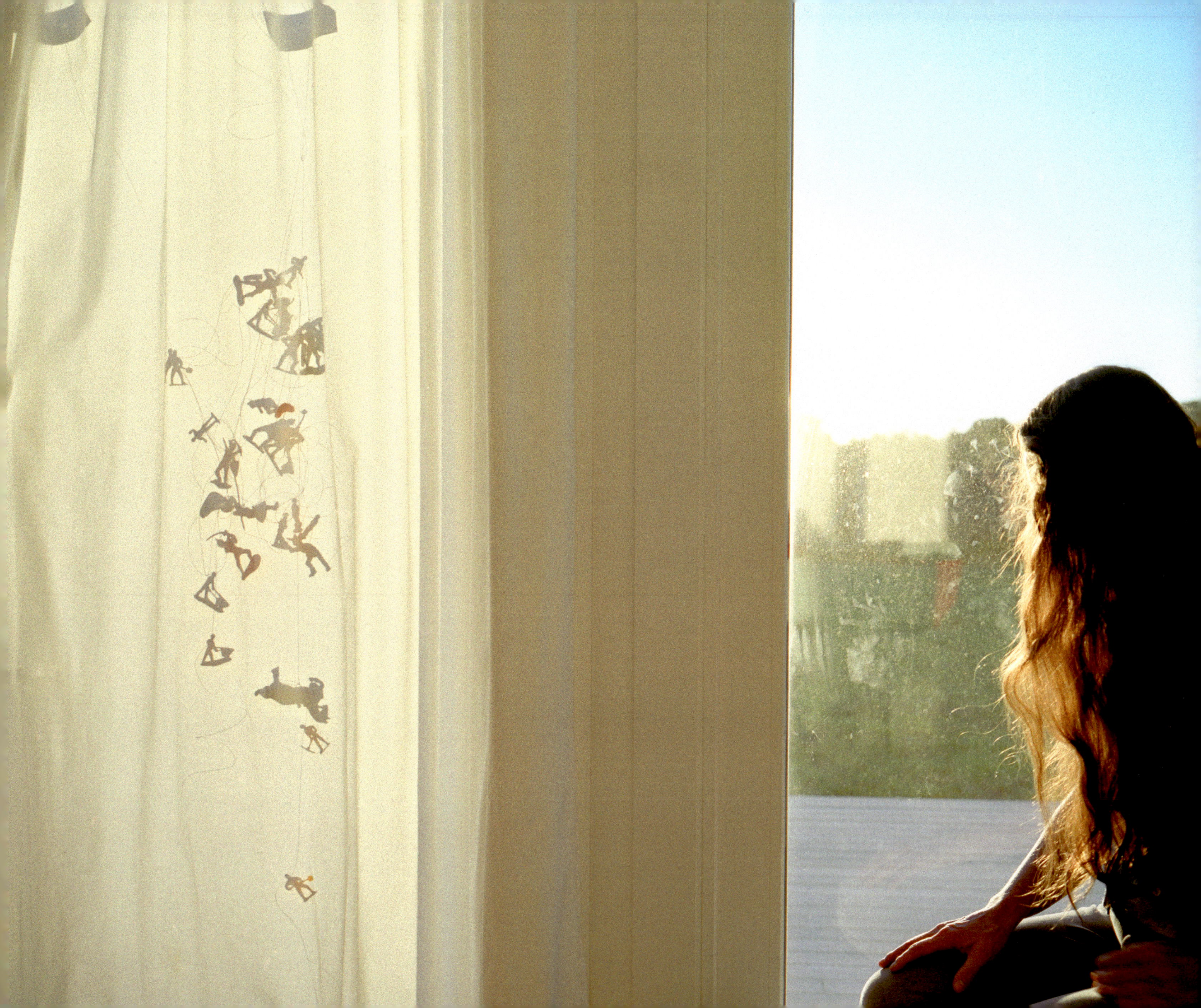

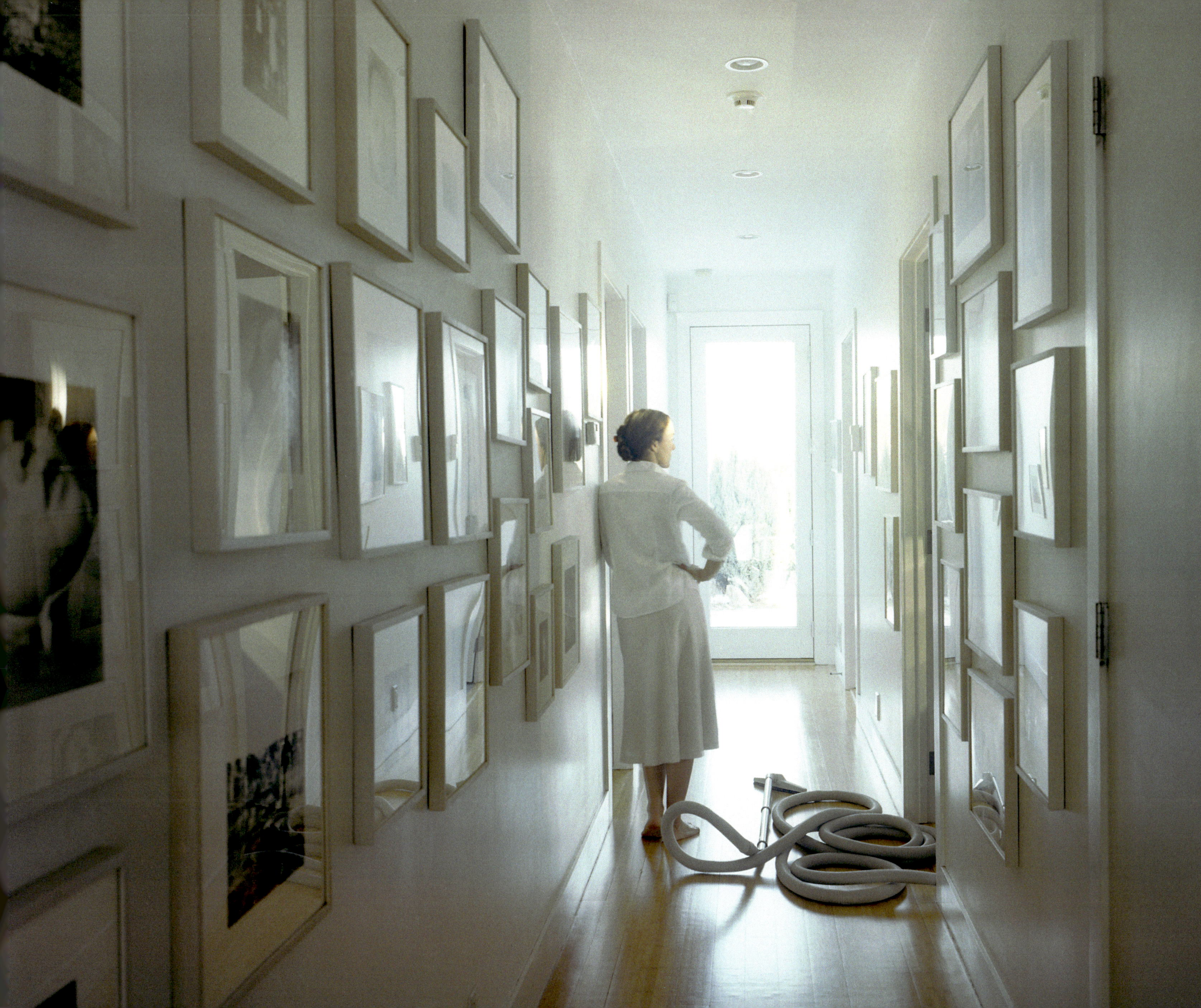

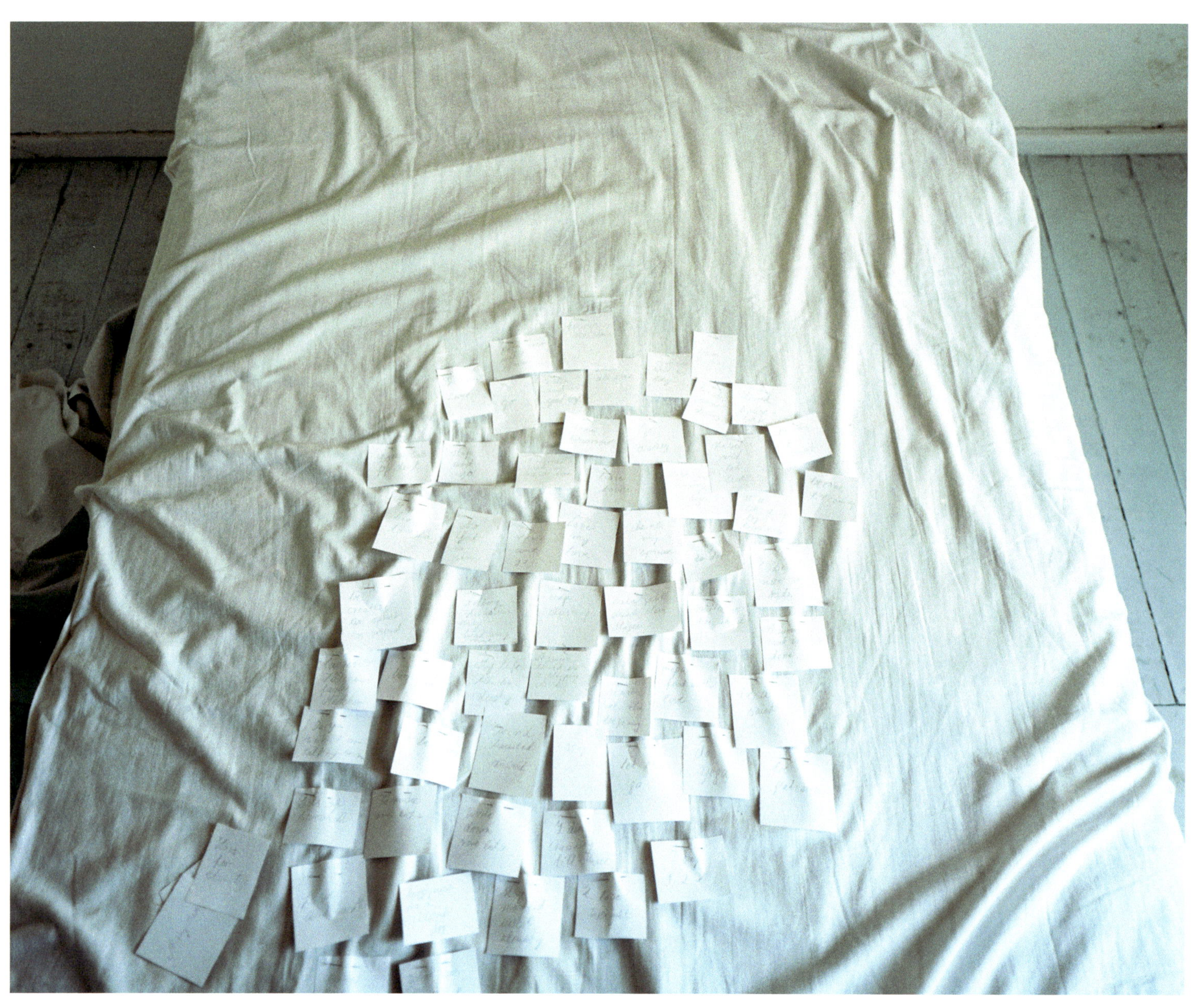

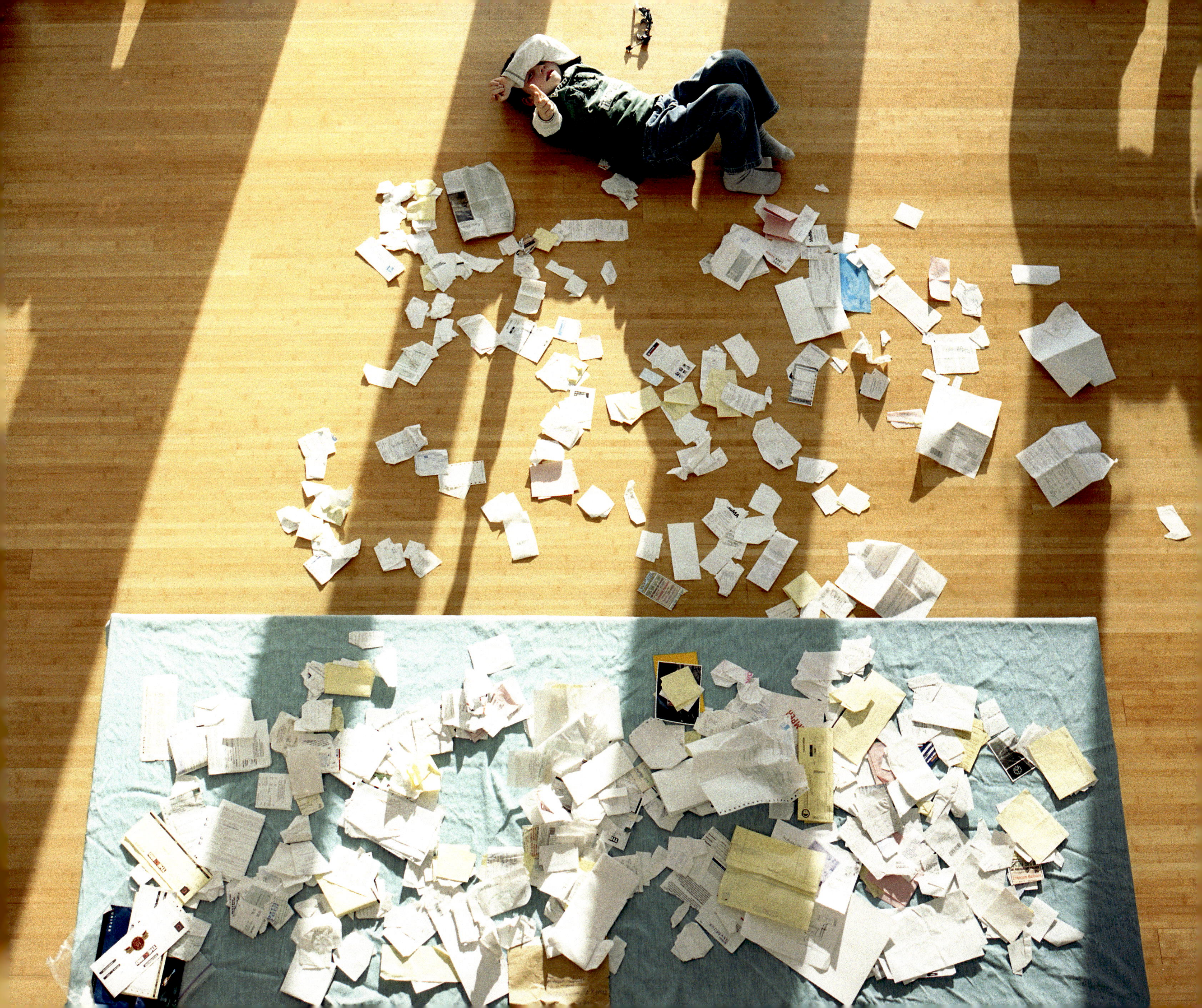

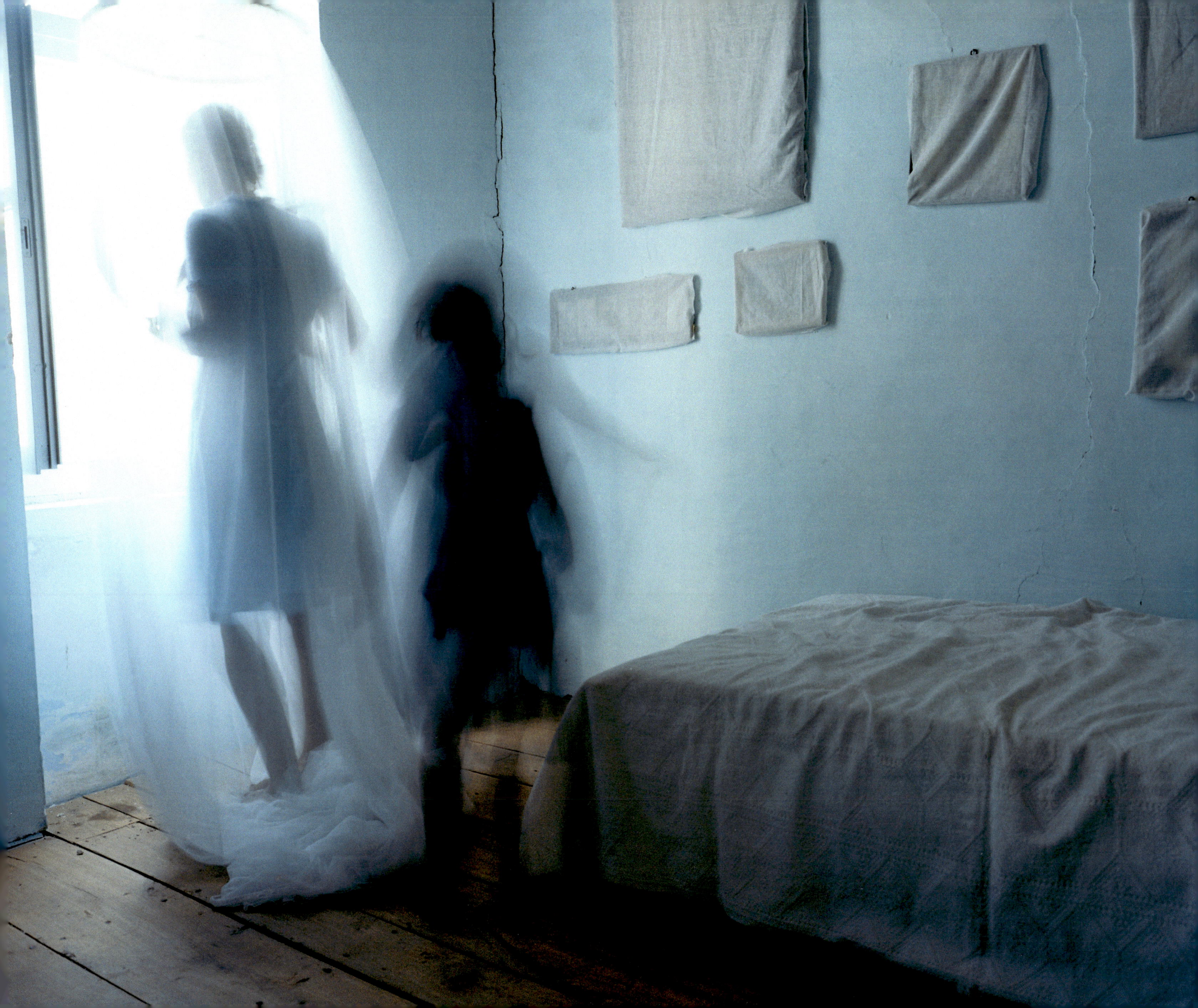

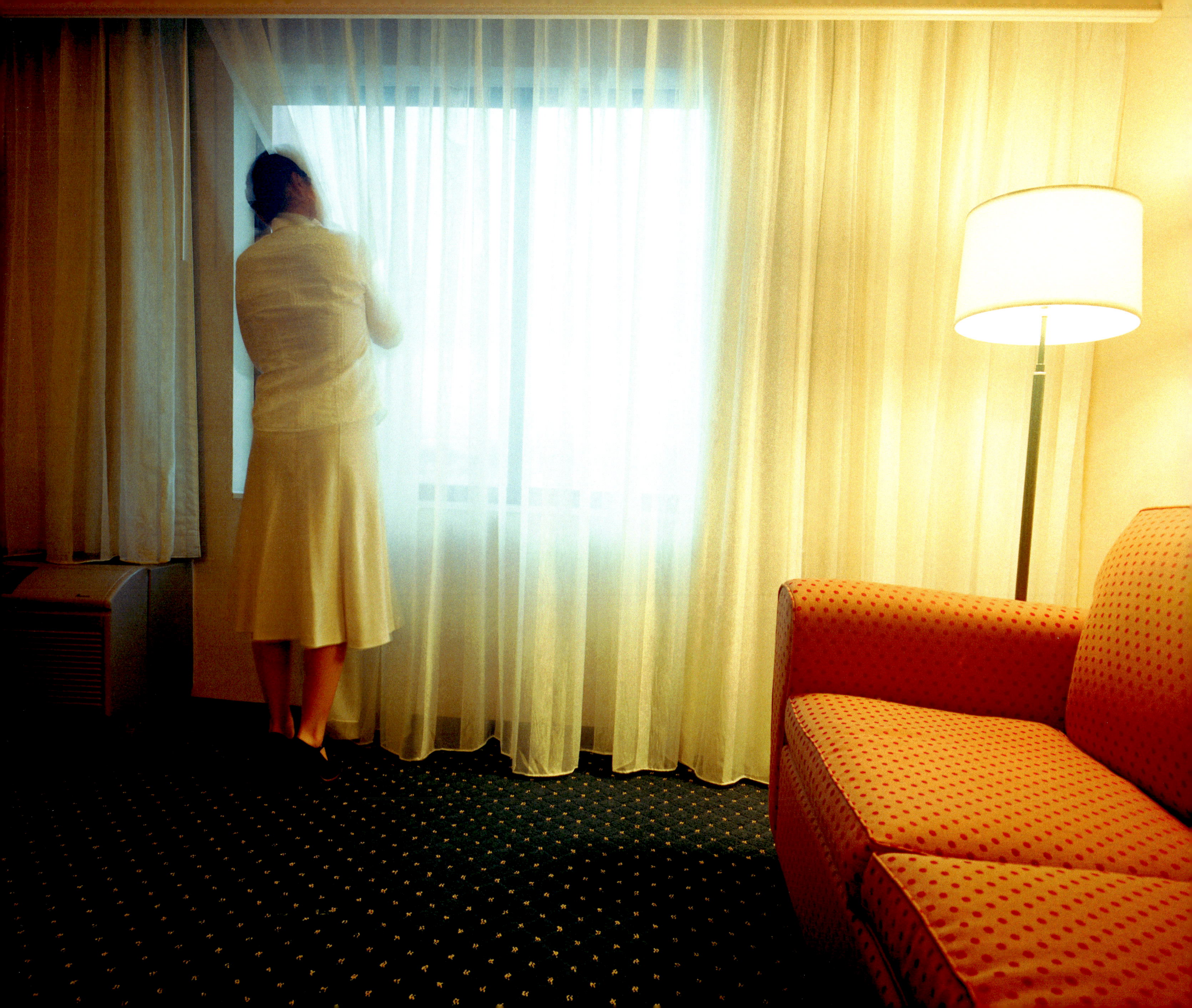

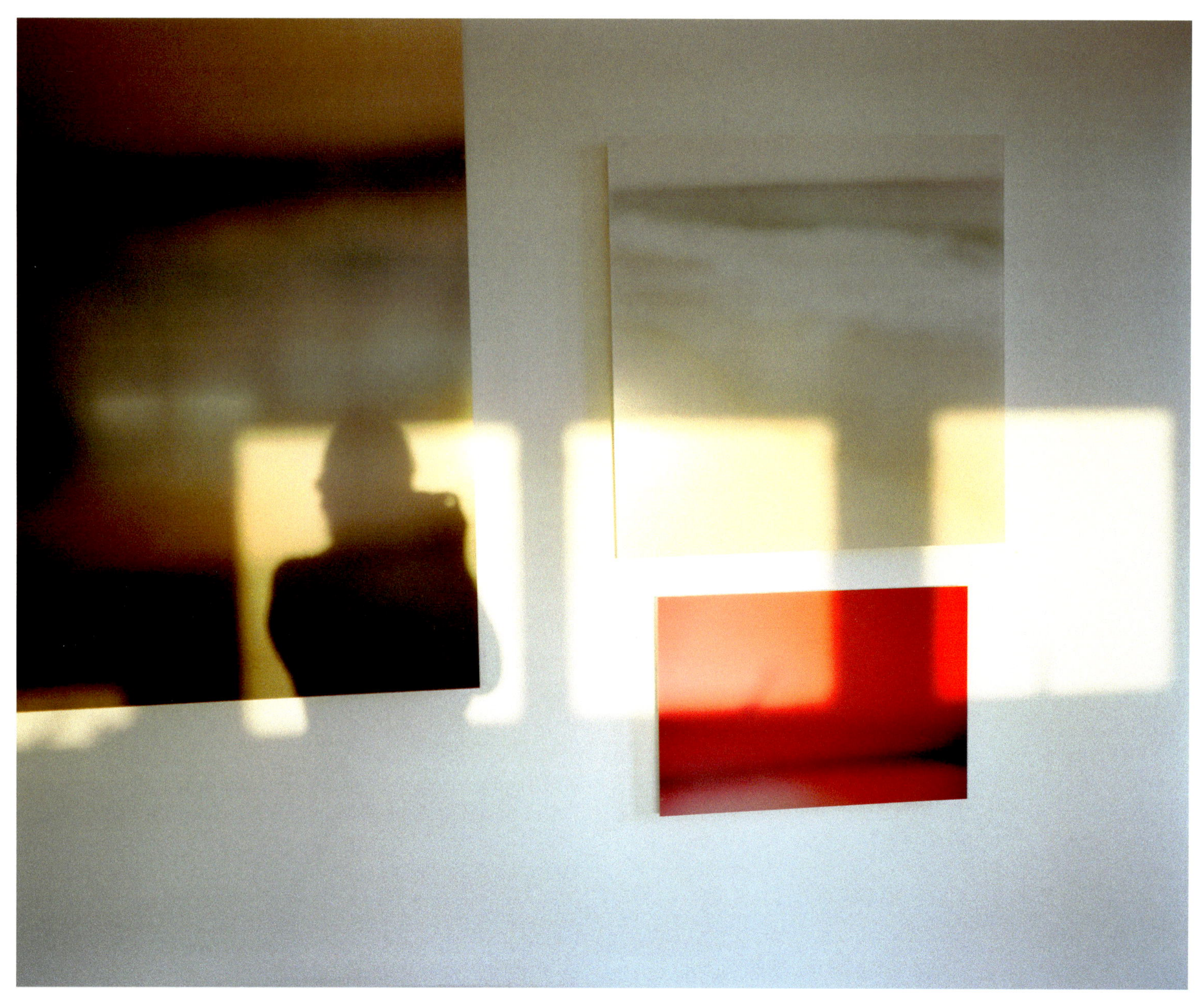

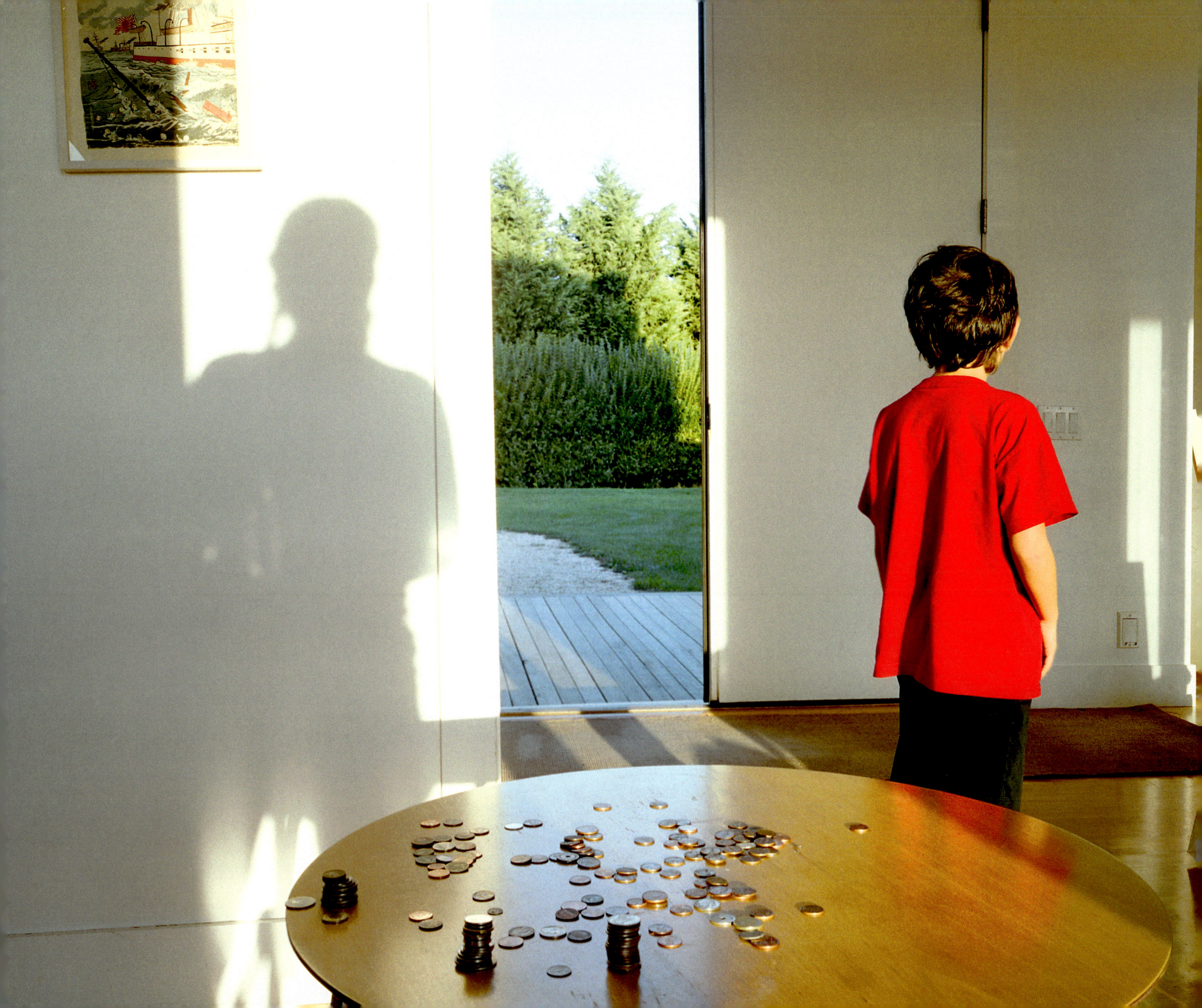

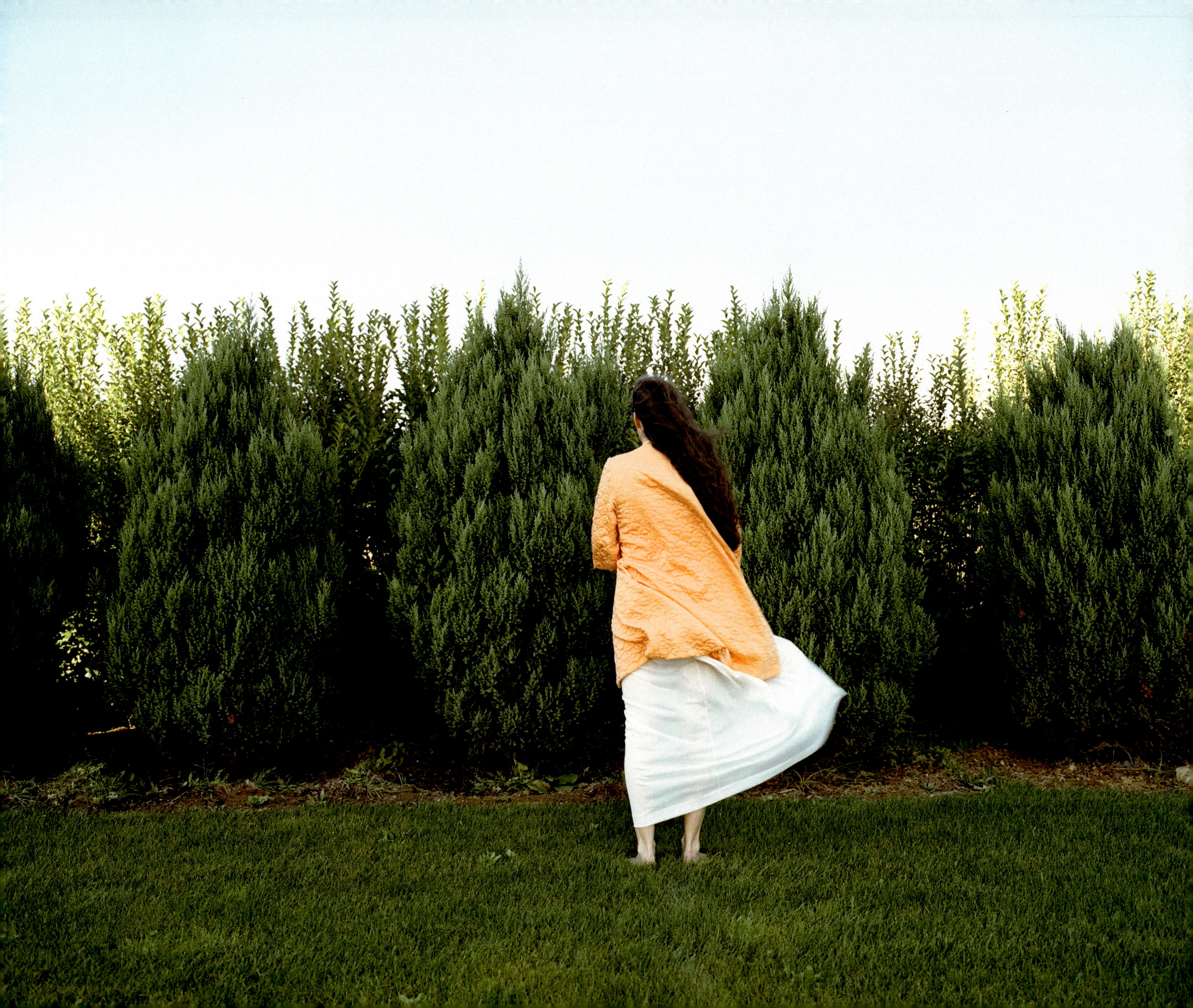

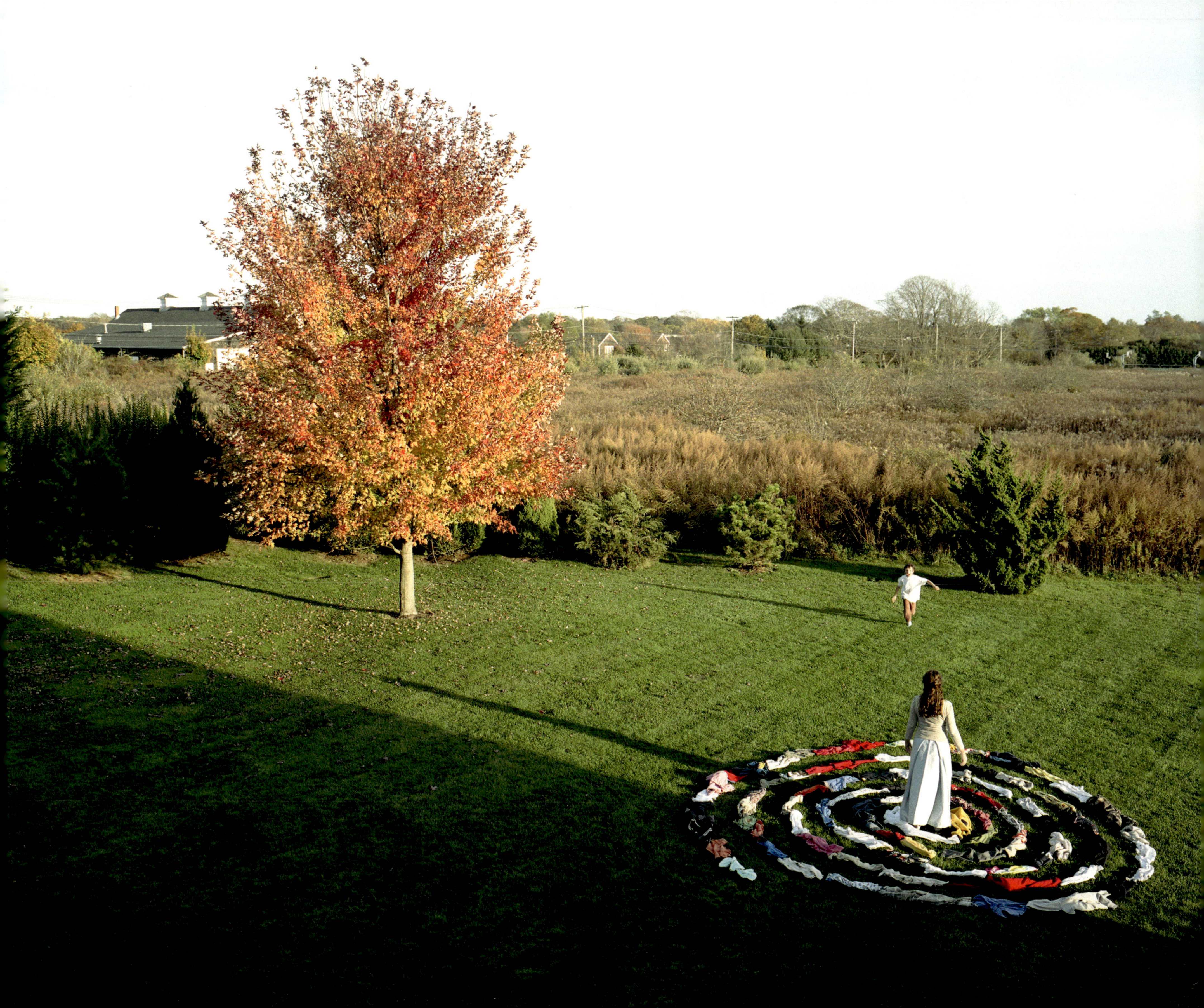

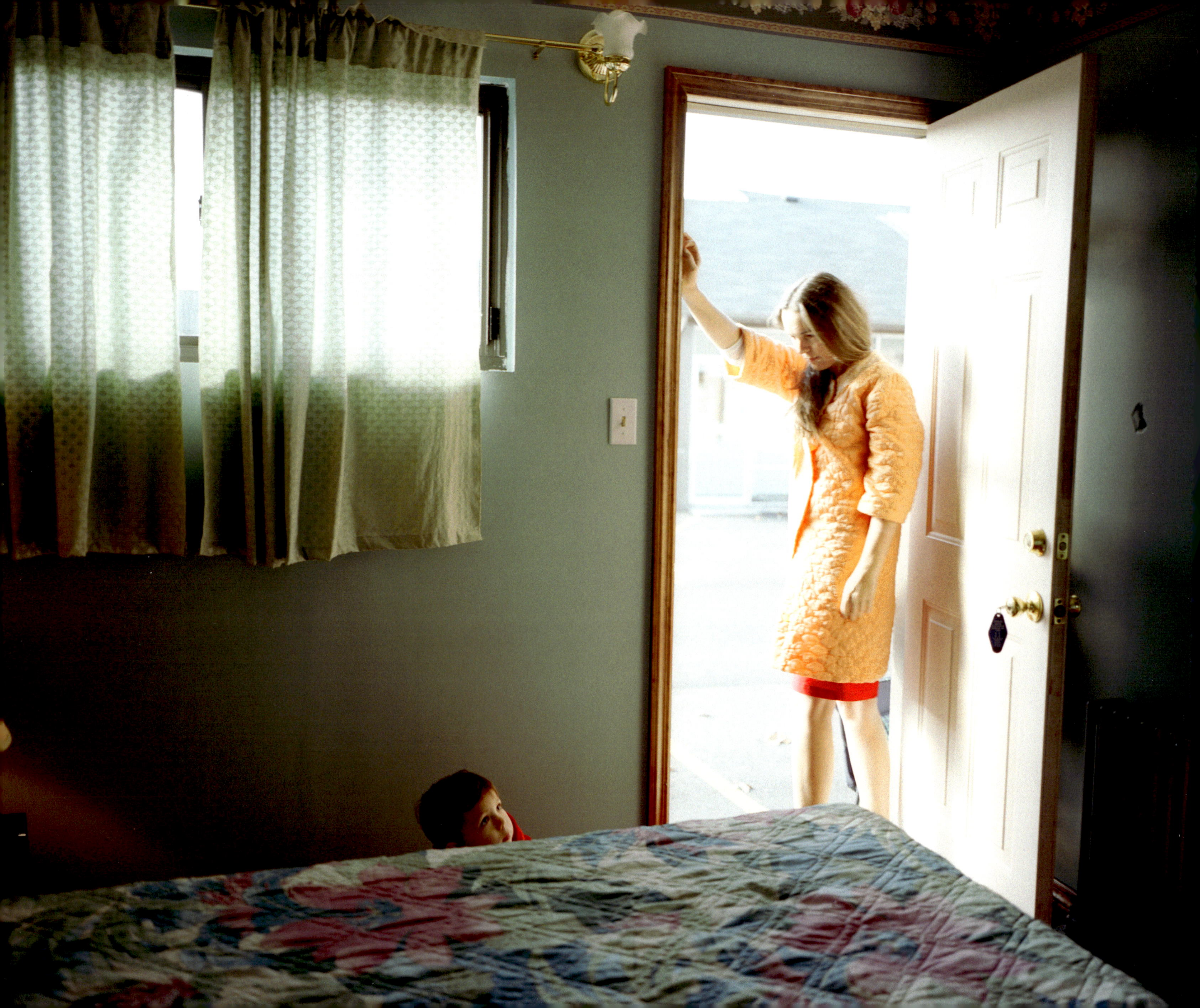

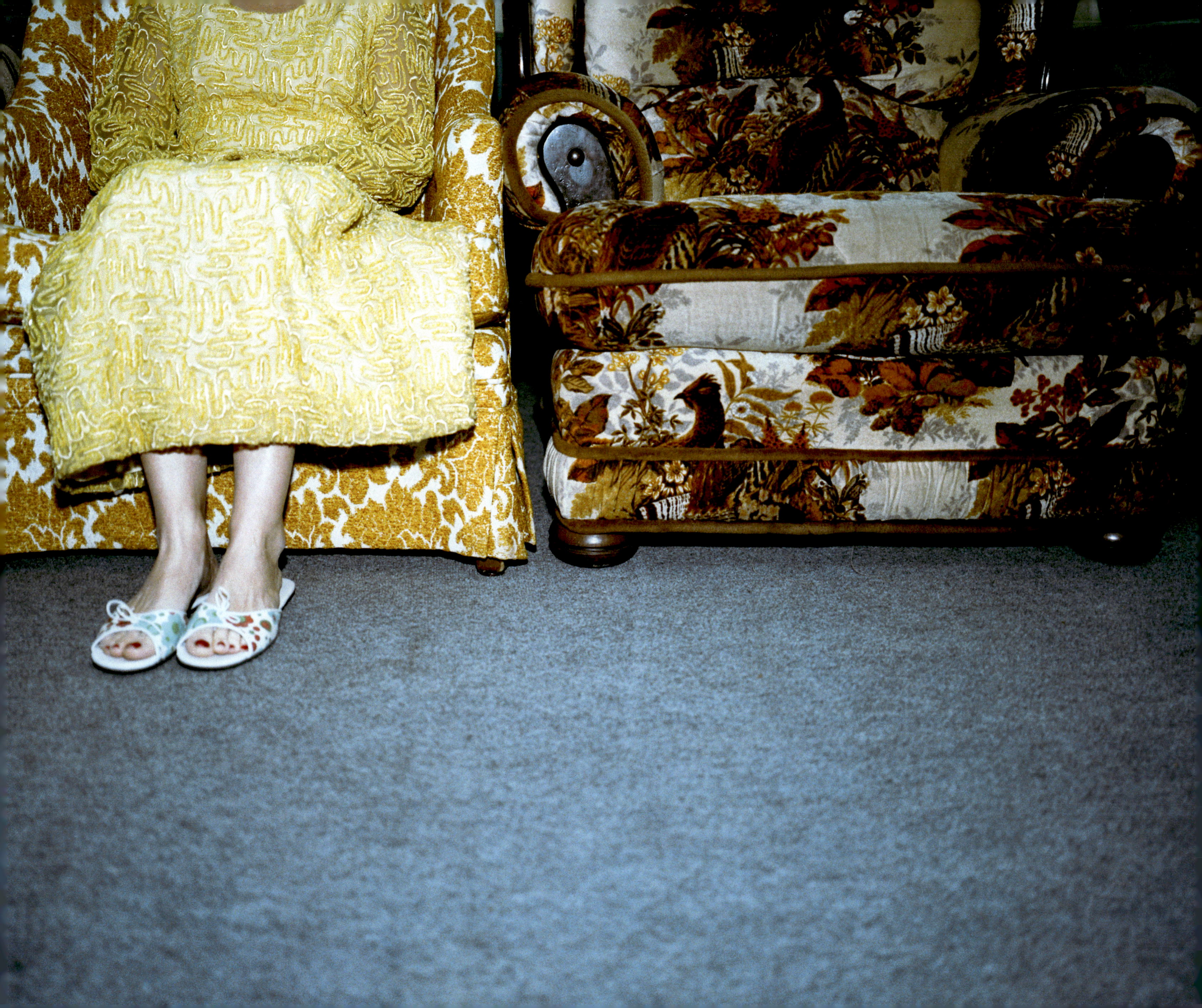

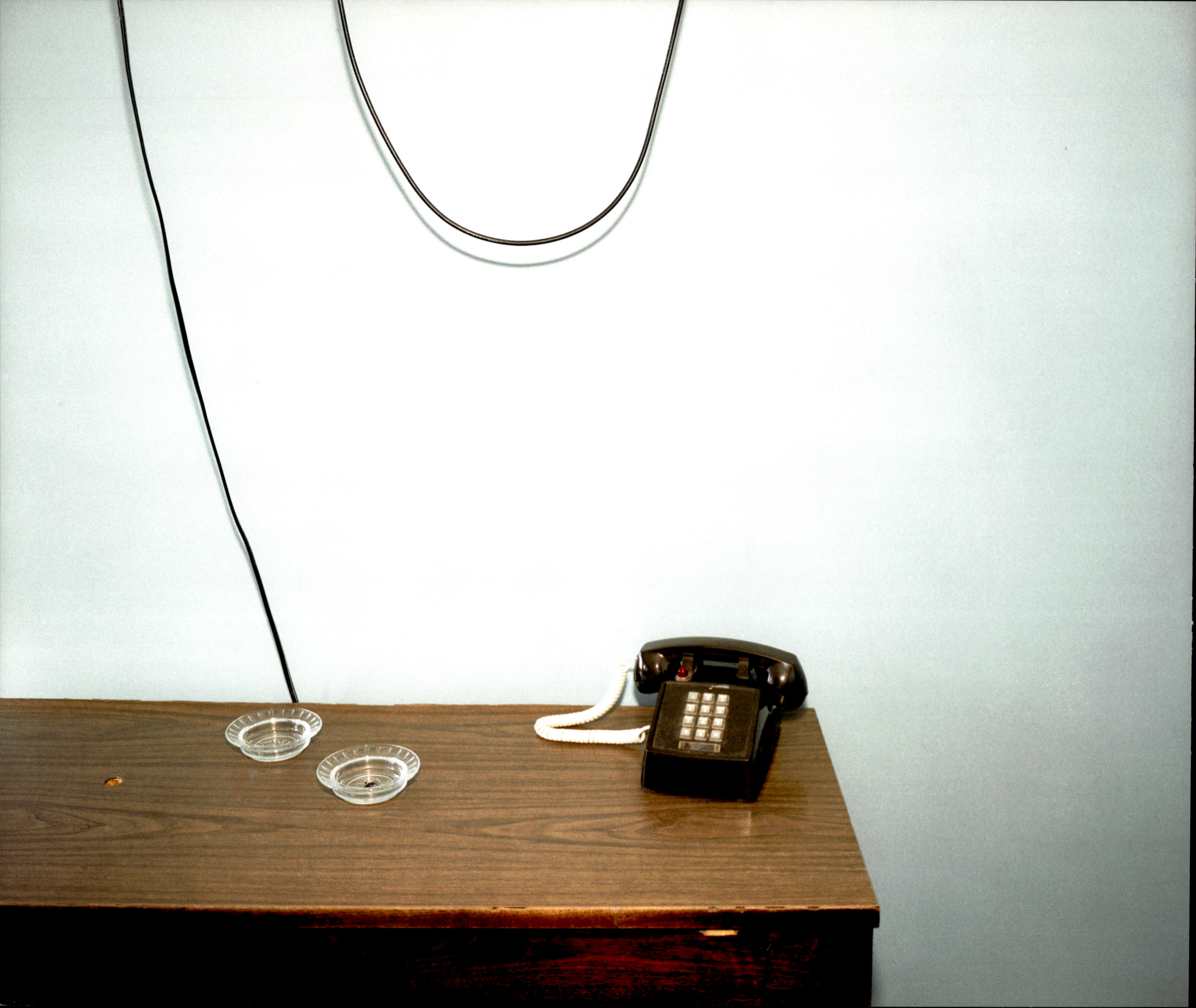

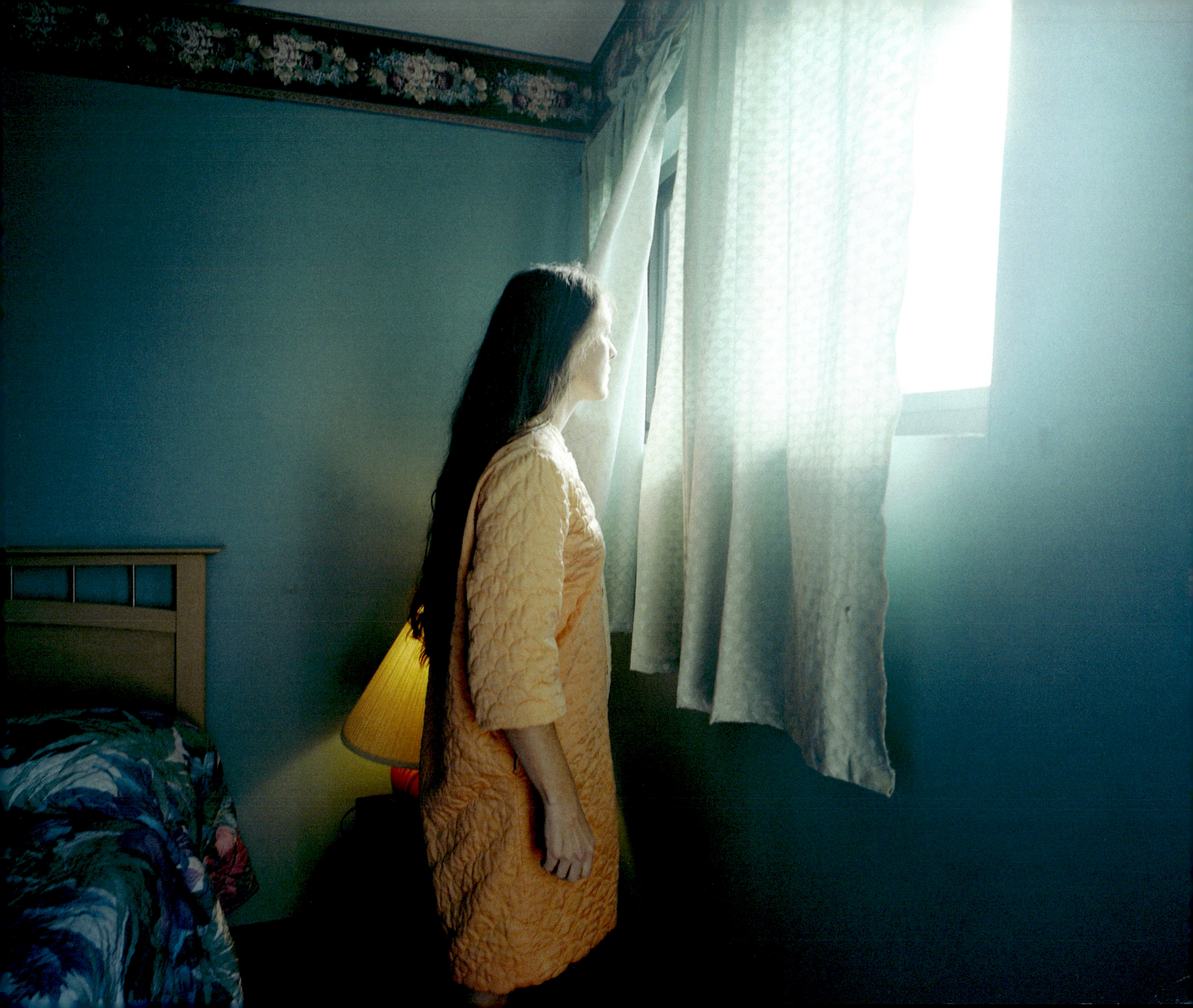

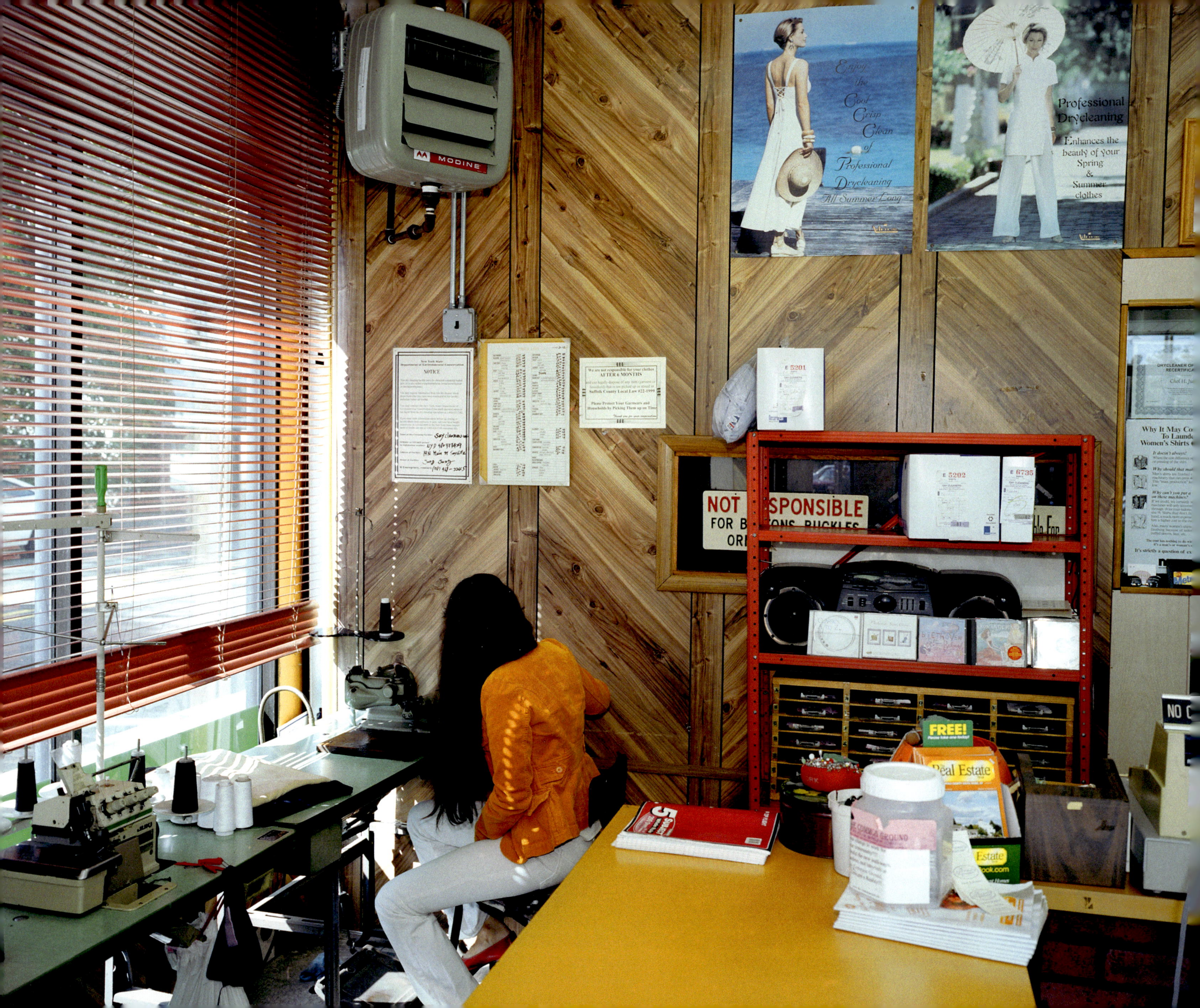

MODINE
Enjoy the Cool Crisp Clean of Professional Drycleaning All Summer Long
Professional Drycleaning
Enhances the beauty of your Spring & Summer clothes
NOTICE
AFTER 6 MONTHS
NOT
SPONSIBLE
FREE!
Real Estate

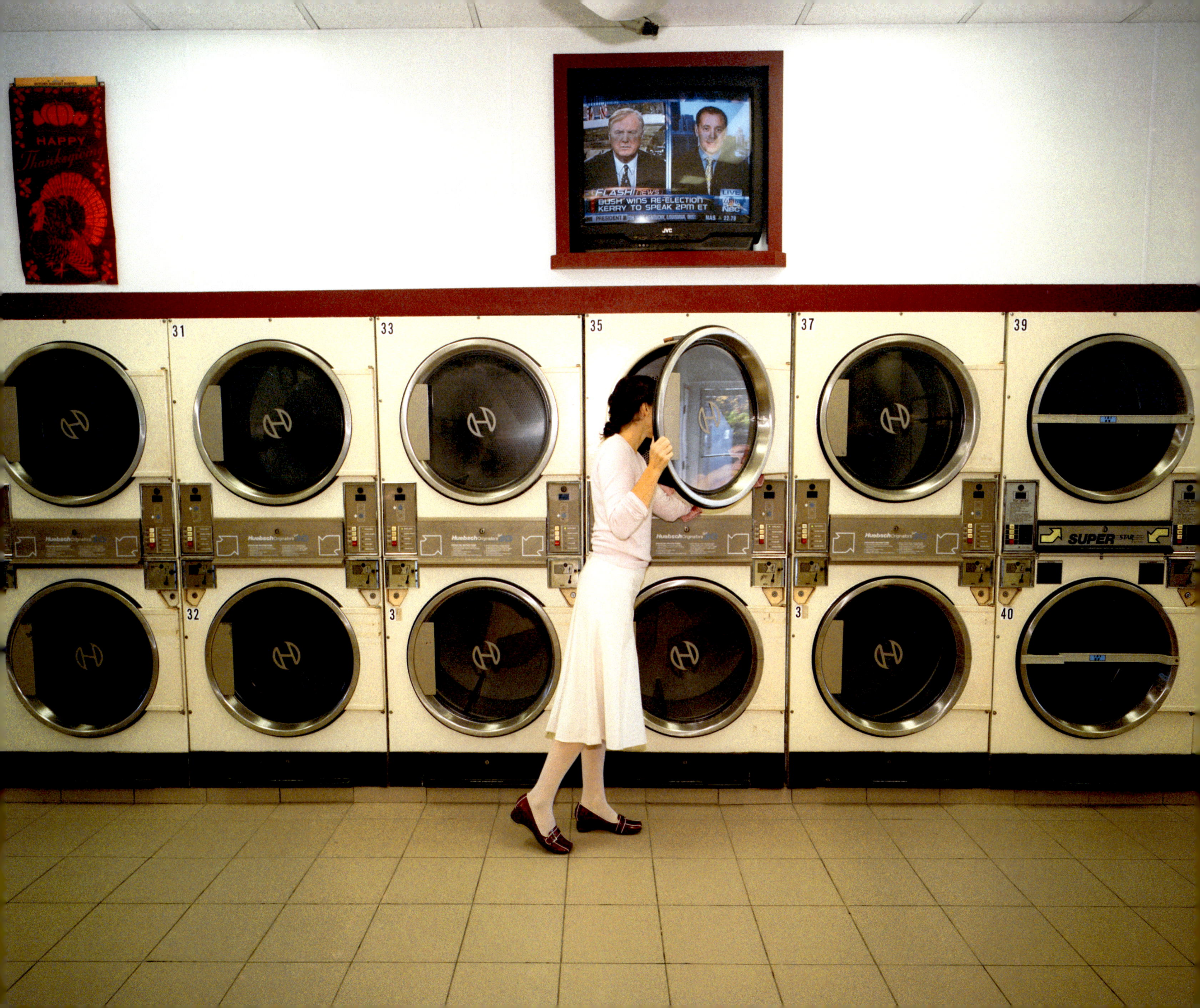
HAPPY
Thanksgiving
FLASH news
BUSH WINS RE-ELECTION
KERRY TO SPEAK 2PM ET
LIVE
JVC
31
33
35
37
39
32
40
Huebsch
SUPER STAR

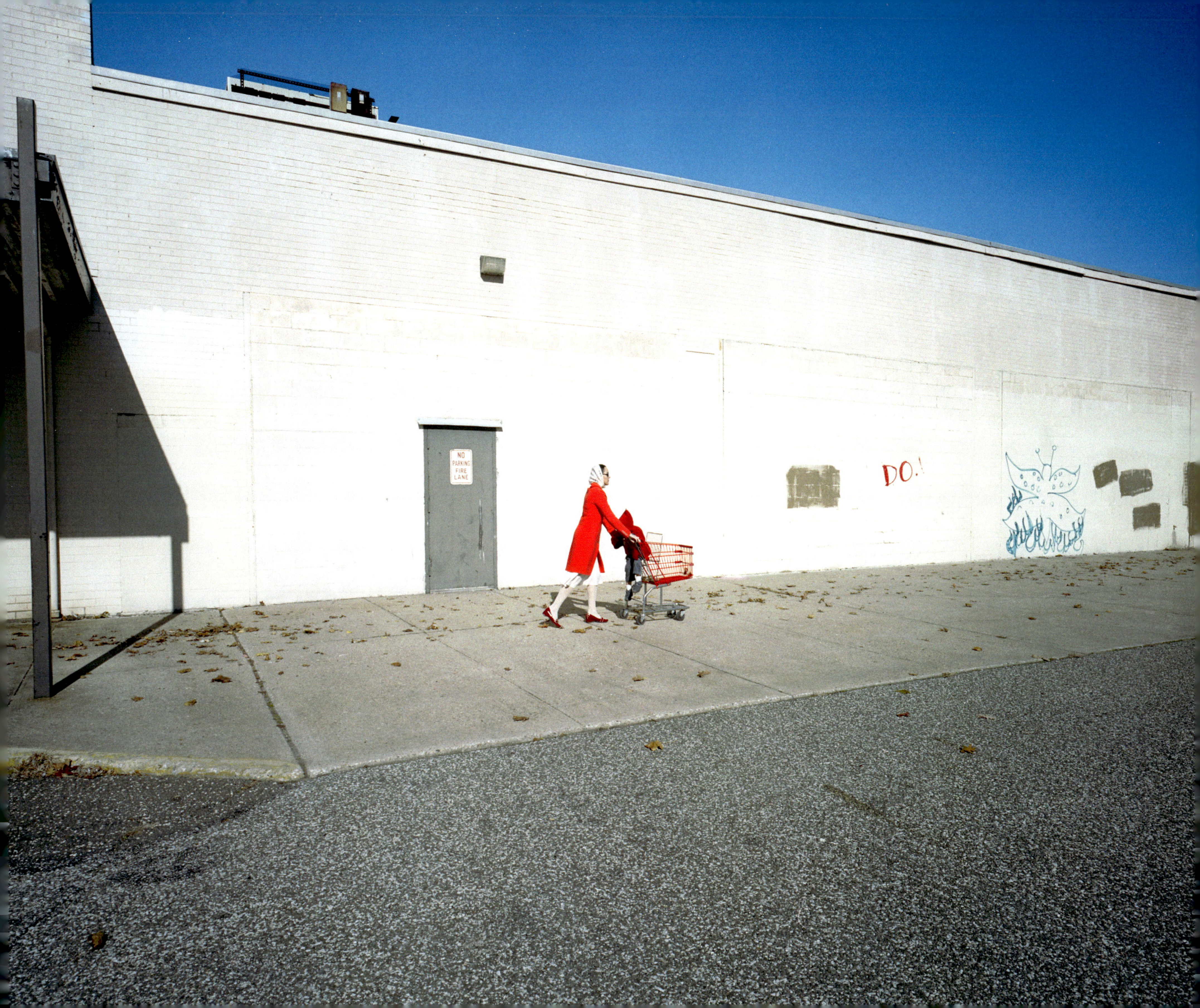
NO PARKING FIRE LANE
DO.!

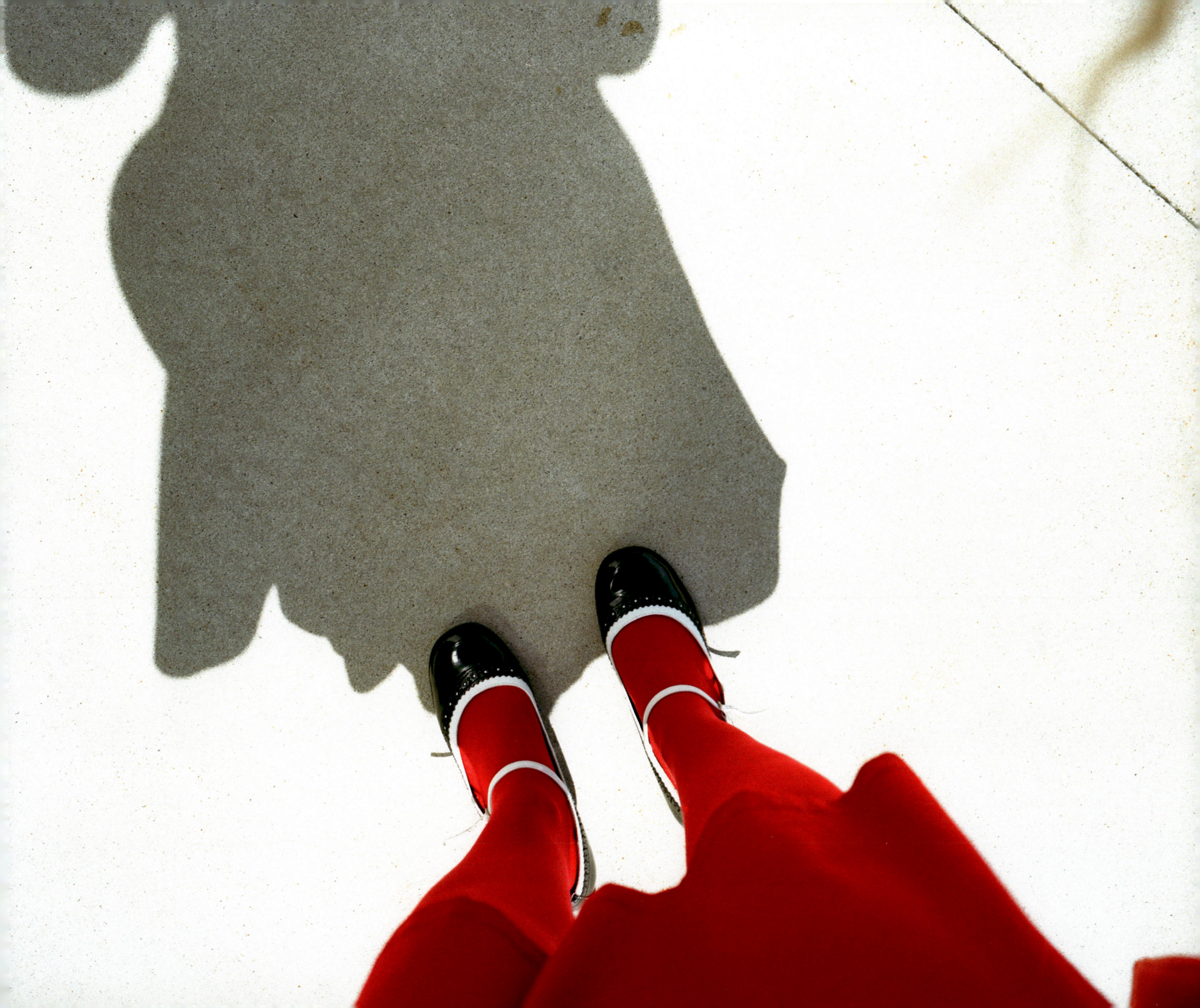

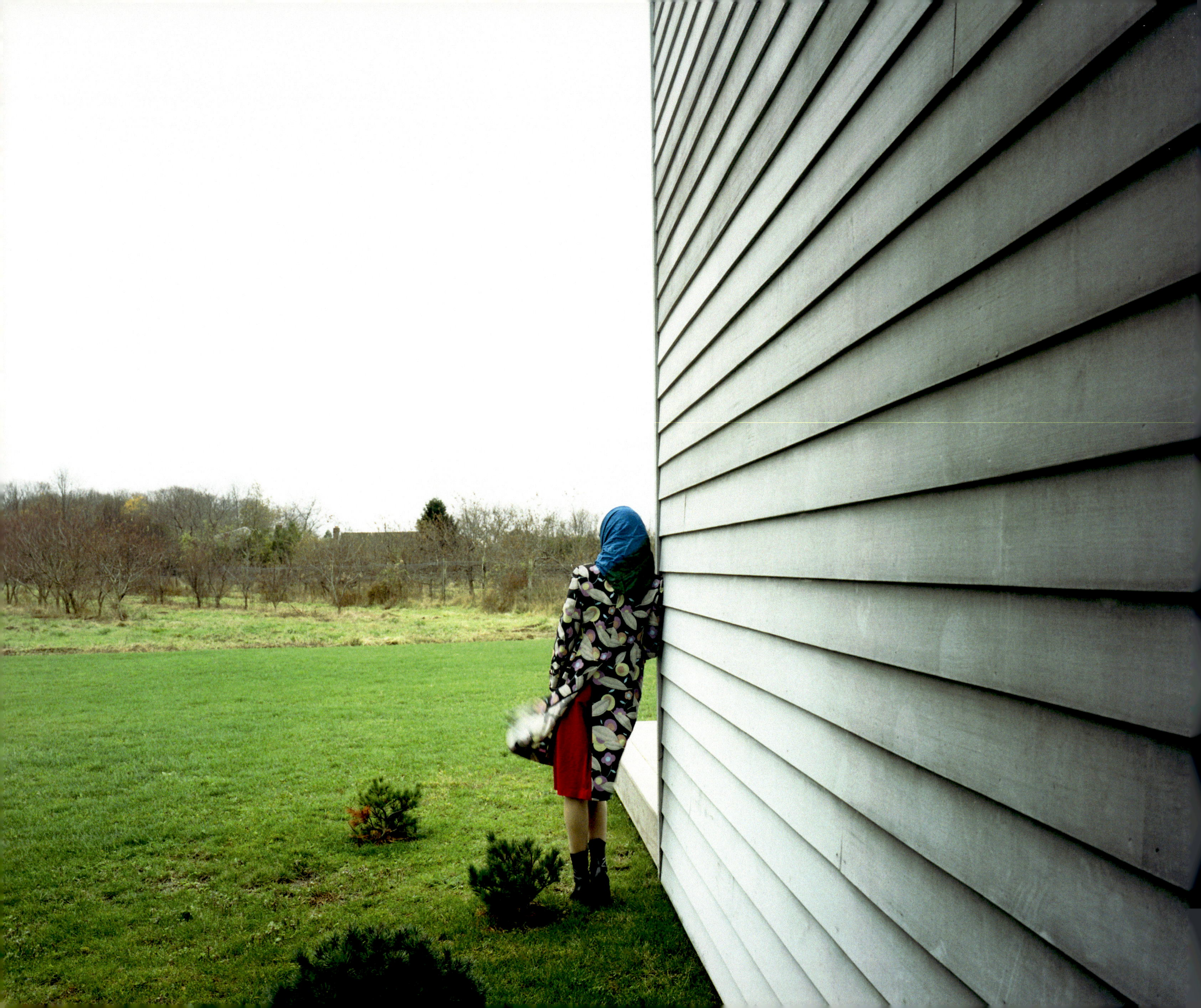

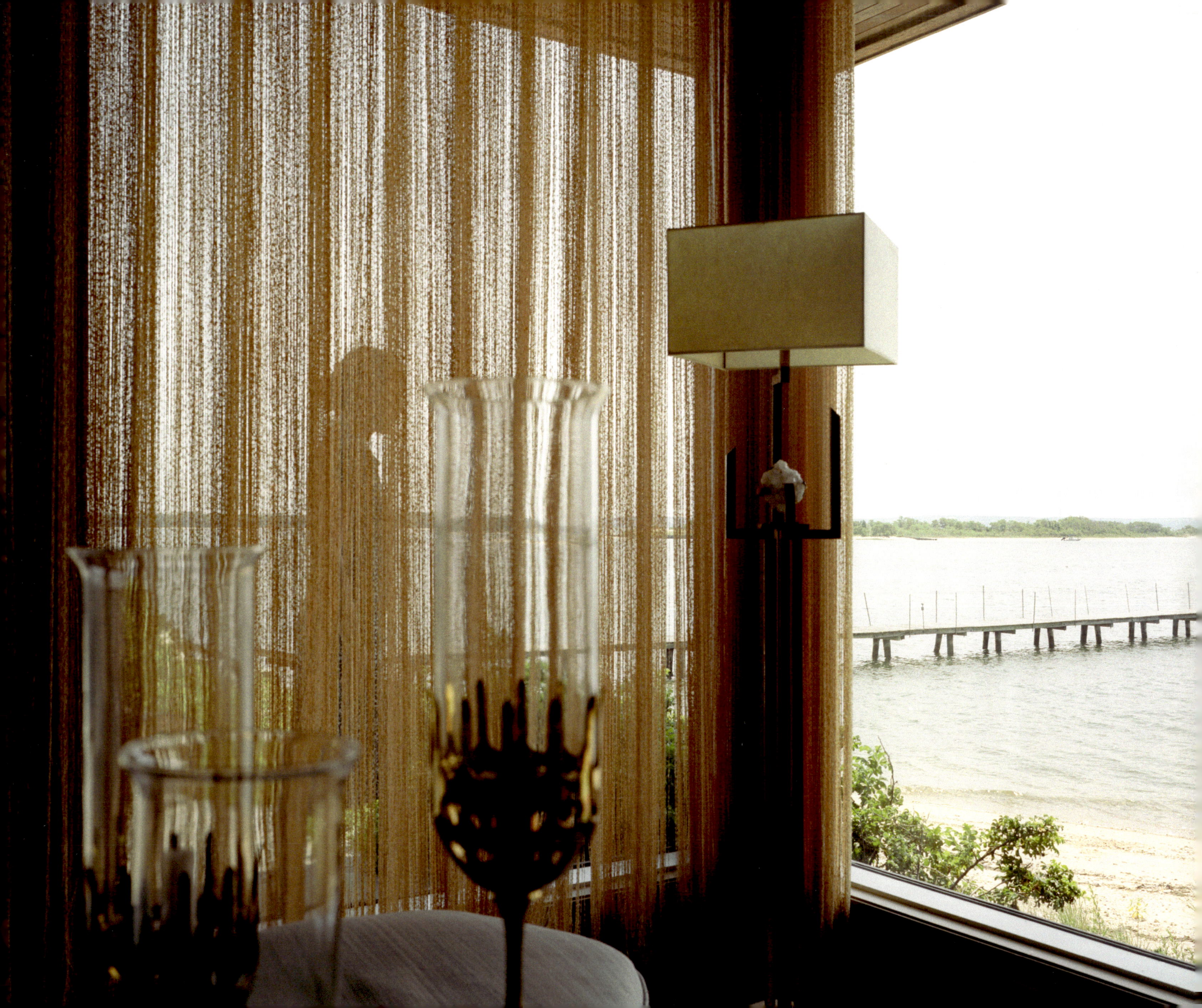

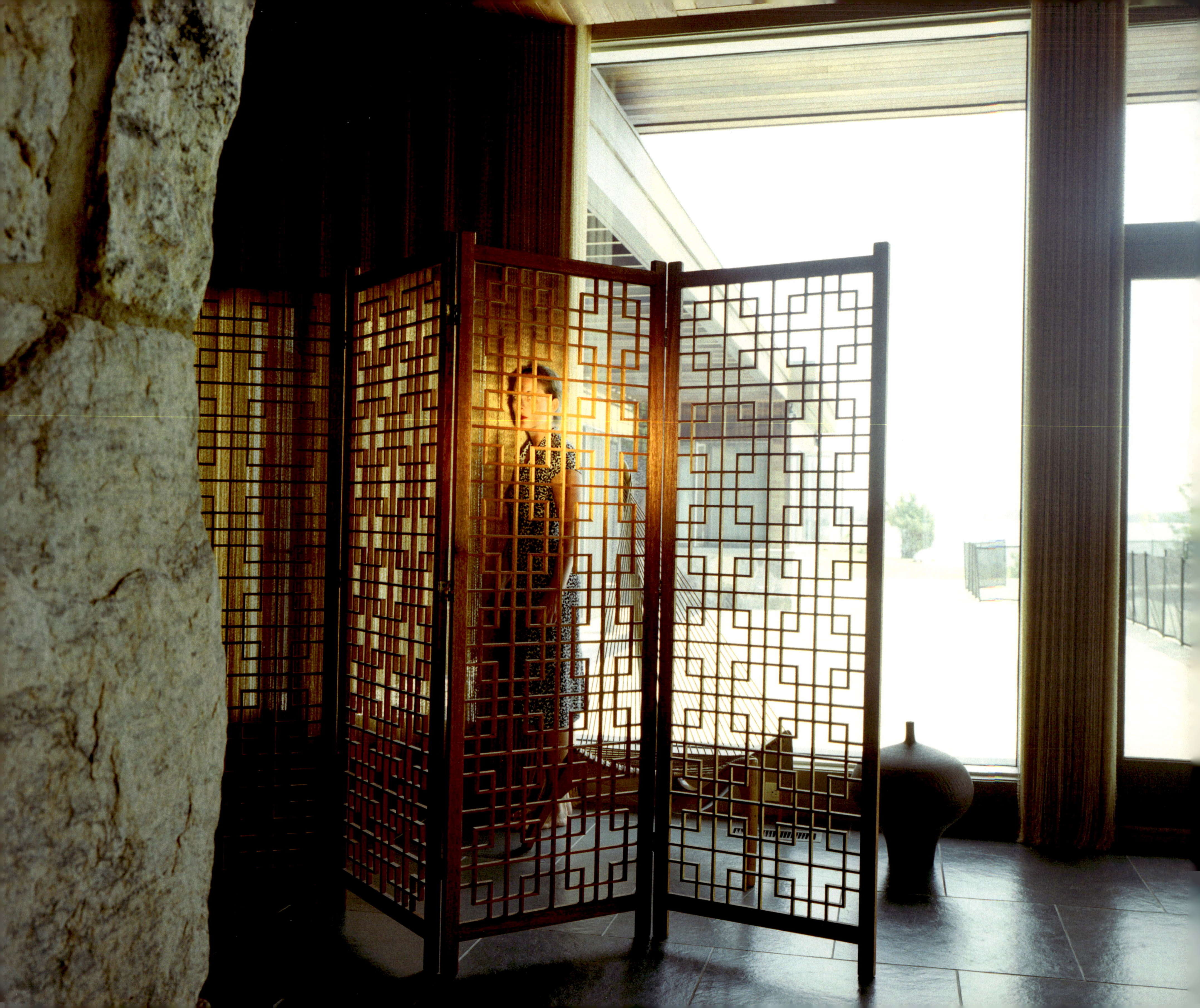

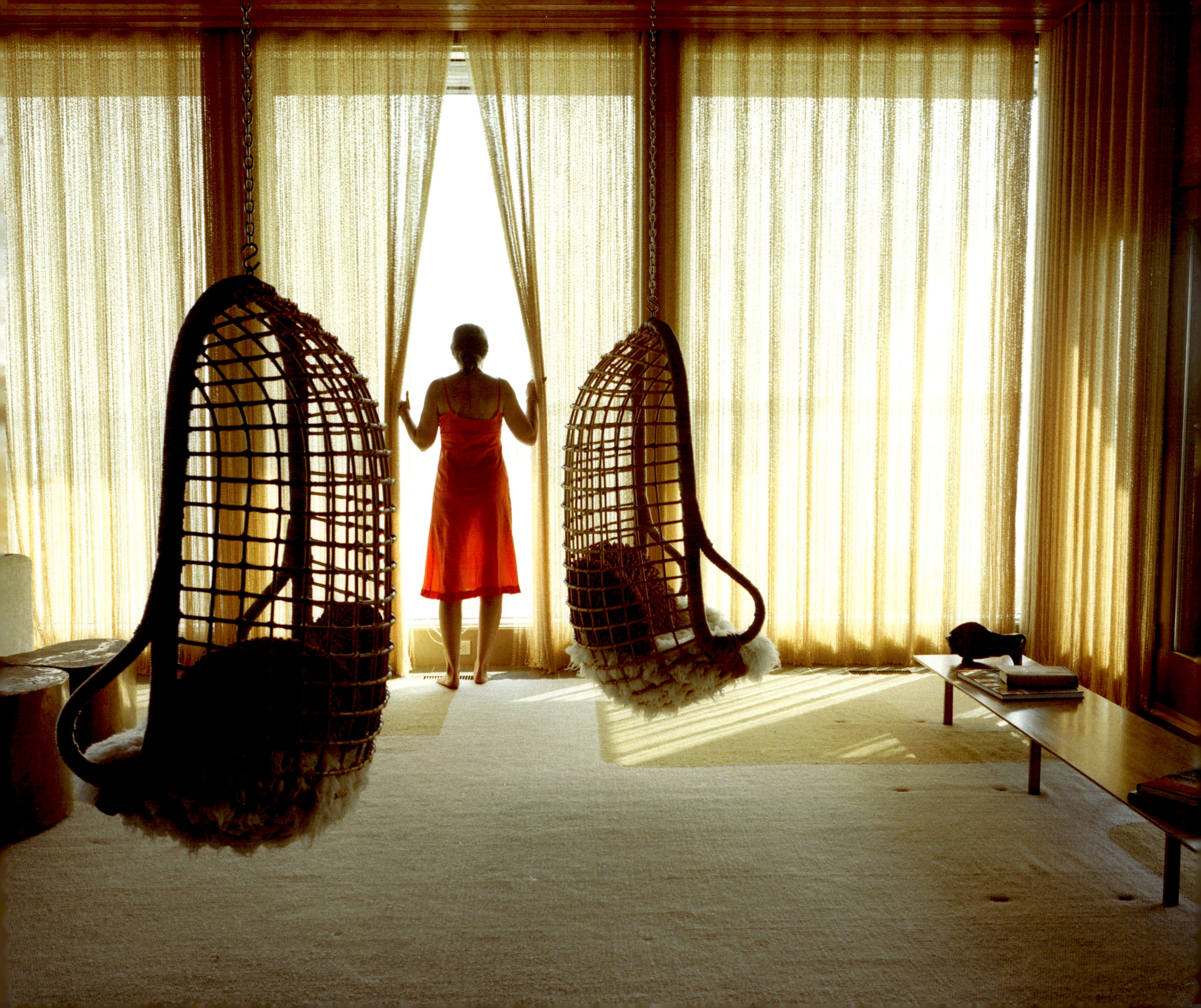

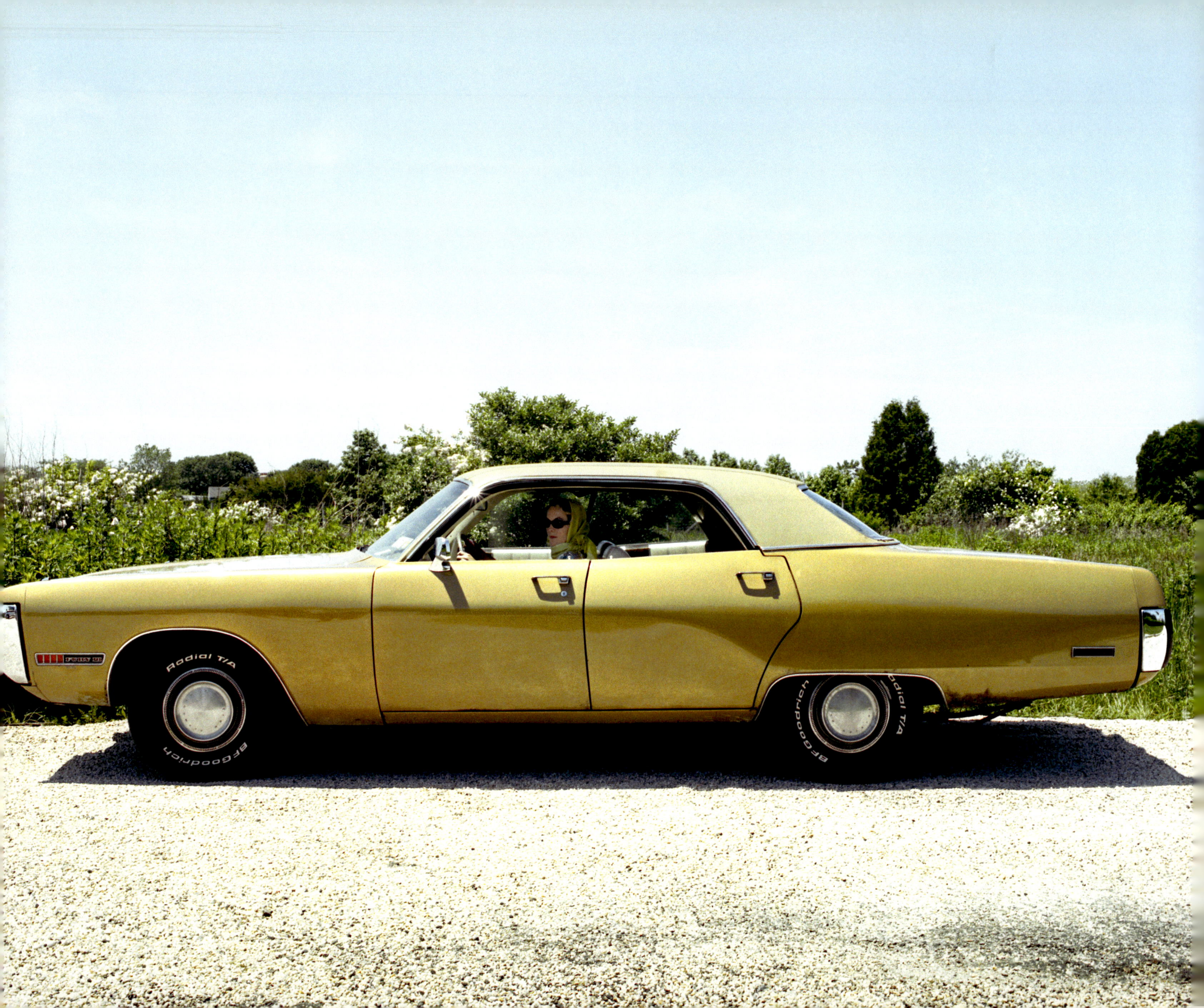
Radial T/A
BFGoodrich

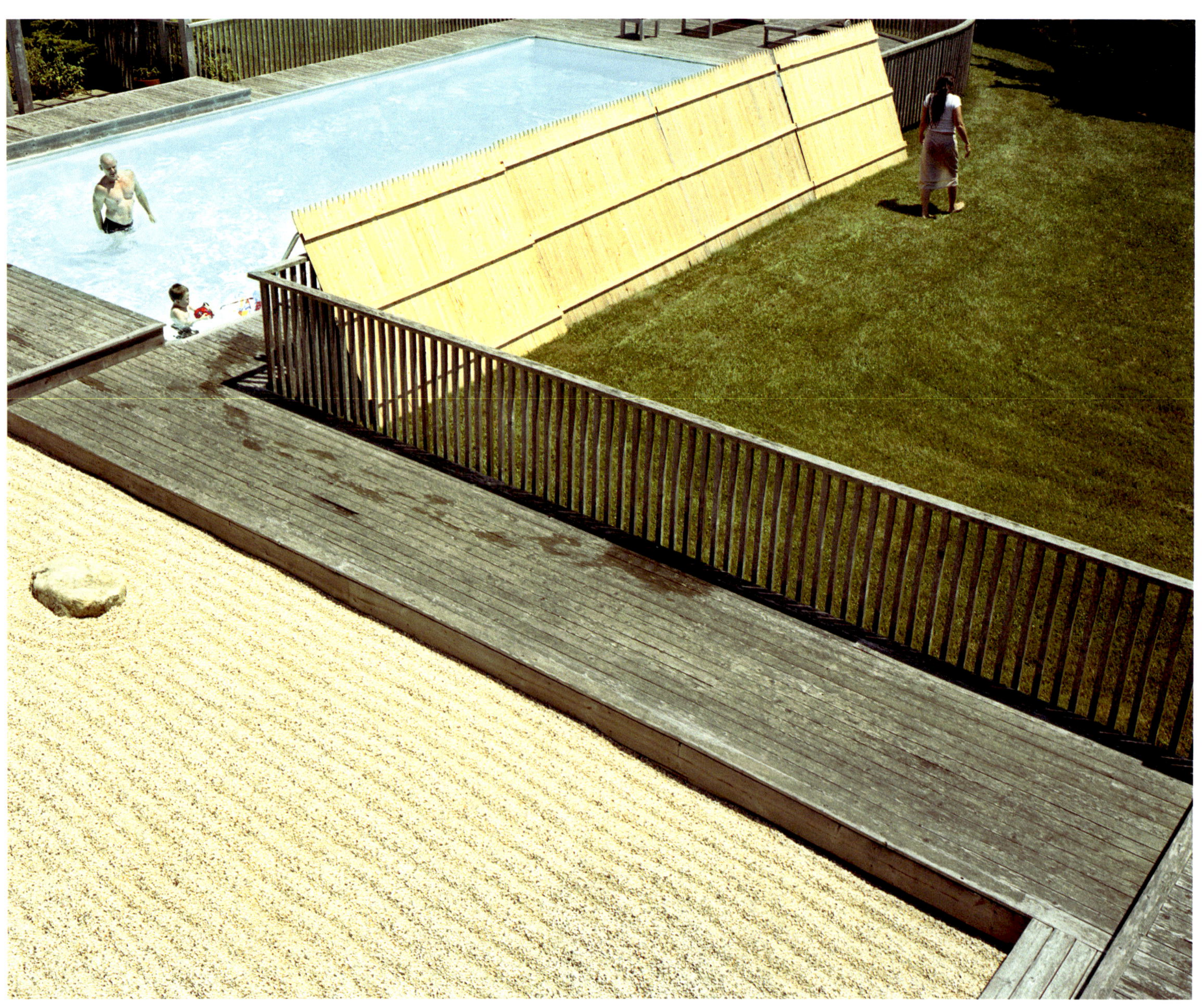

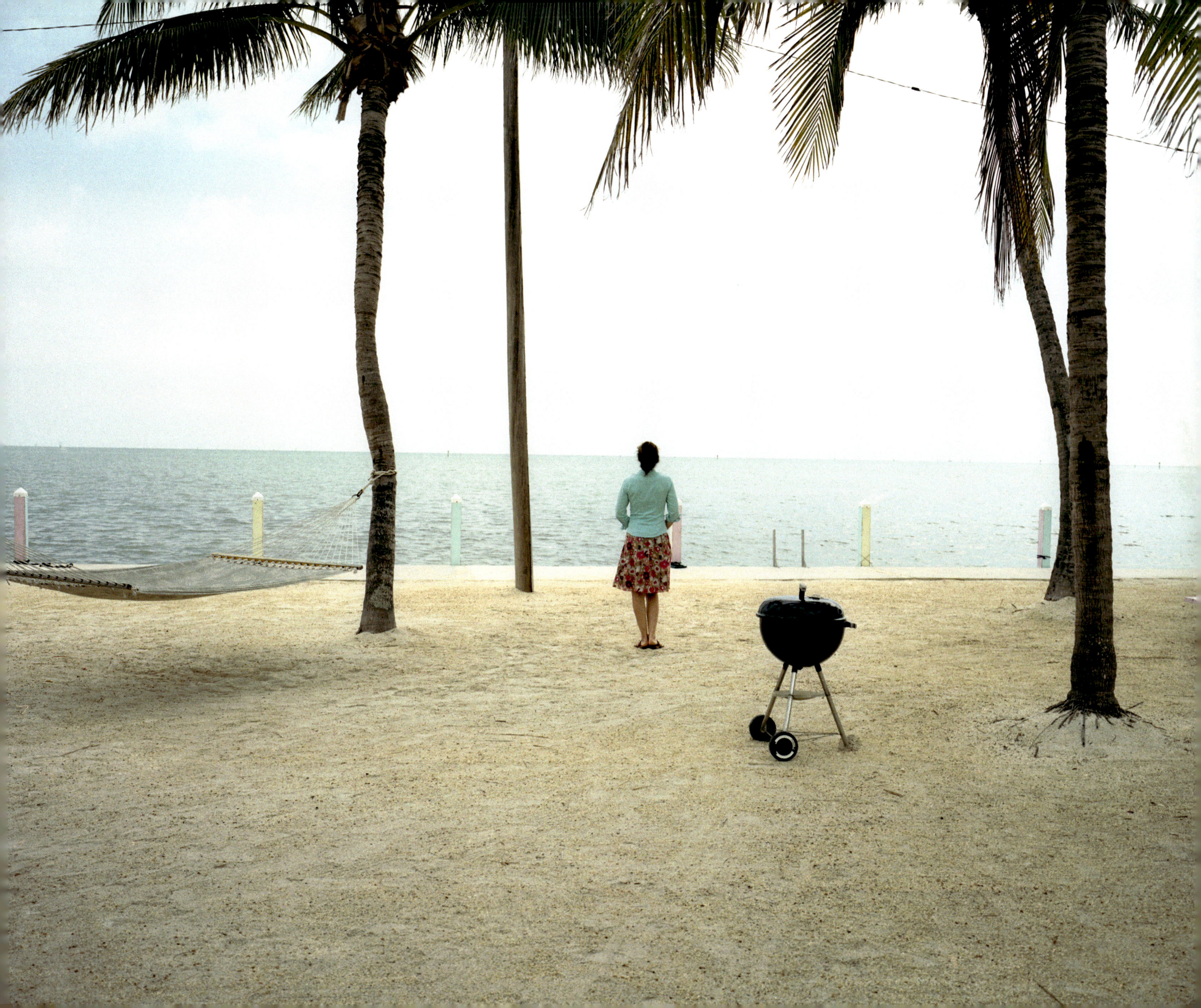

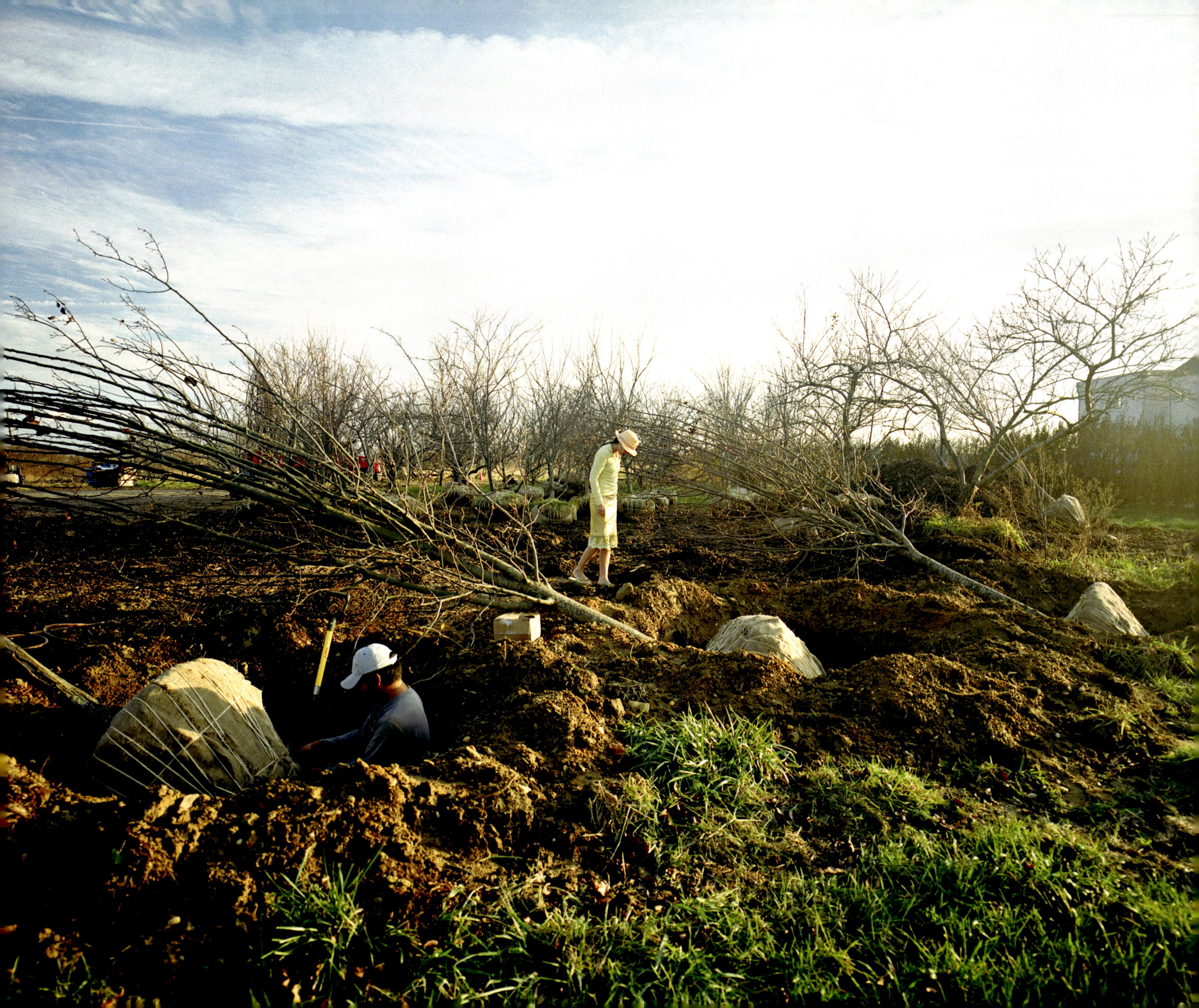

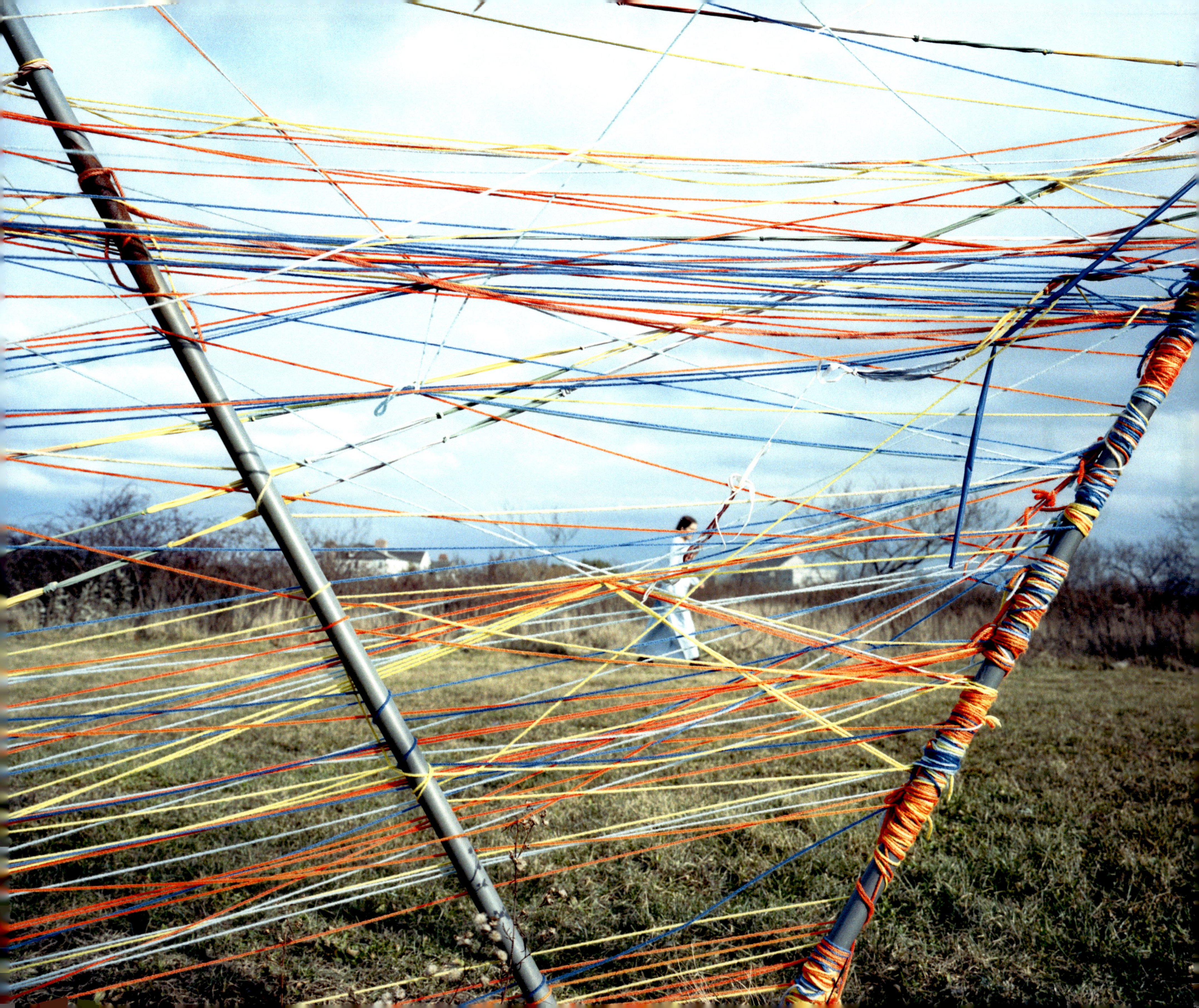

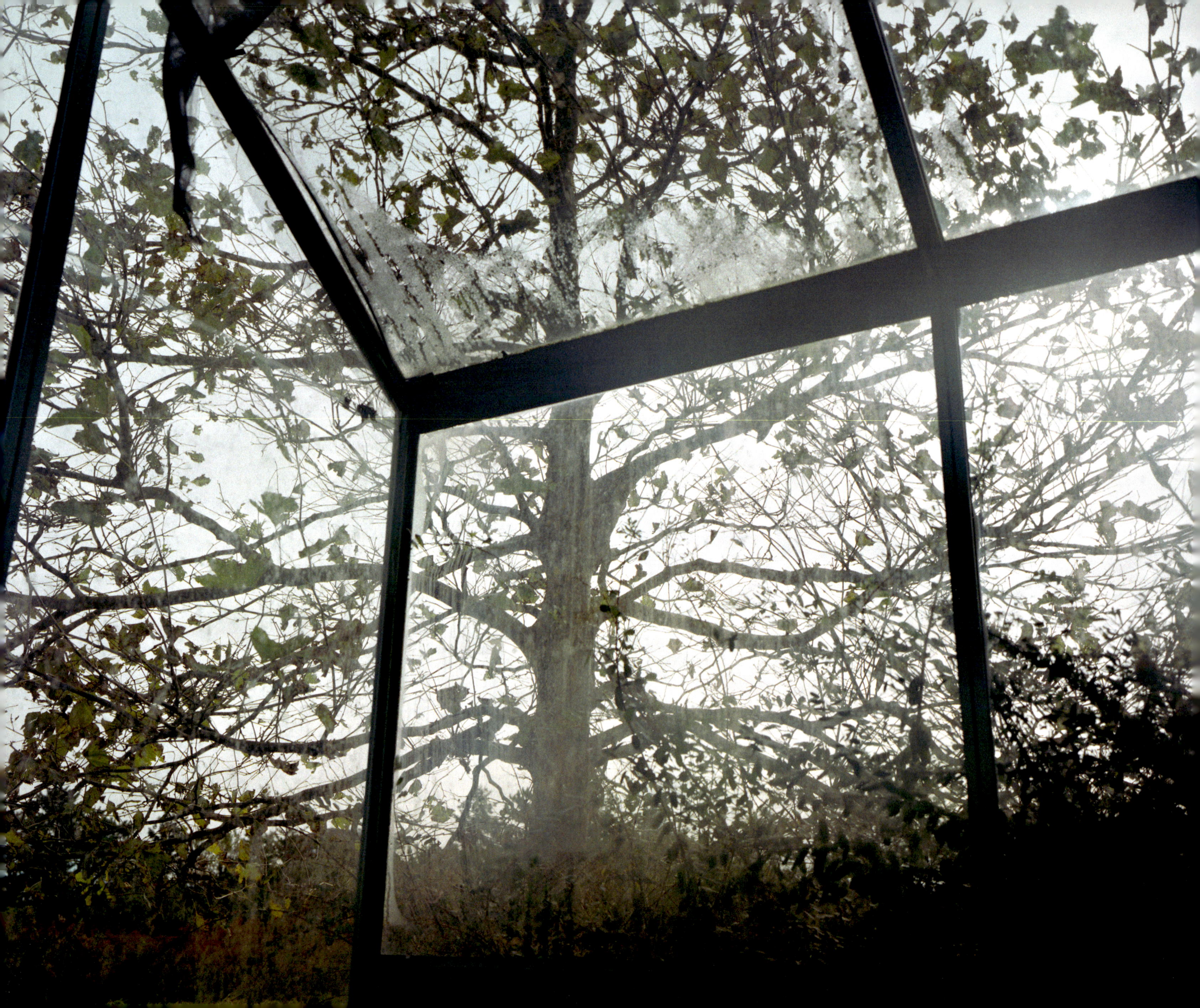

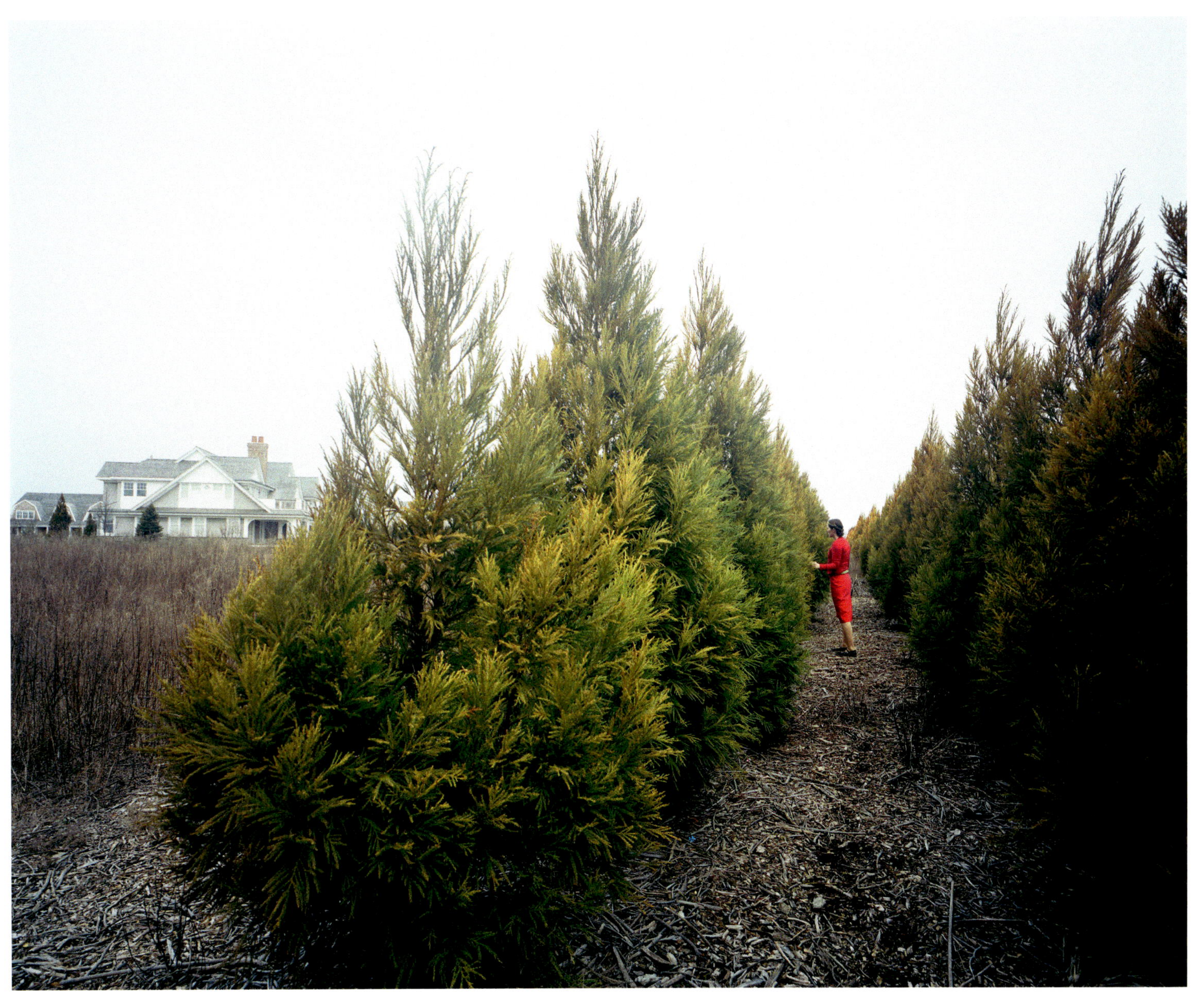

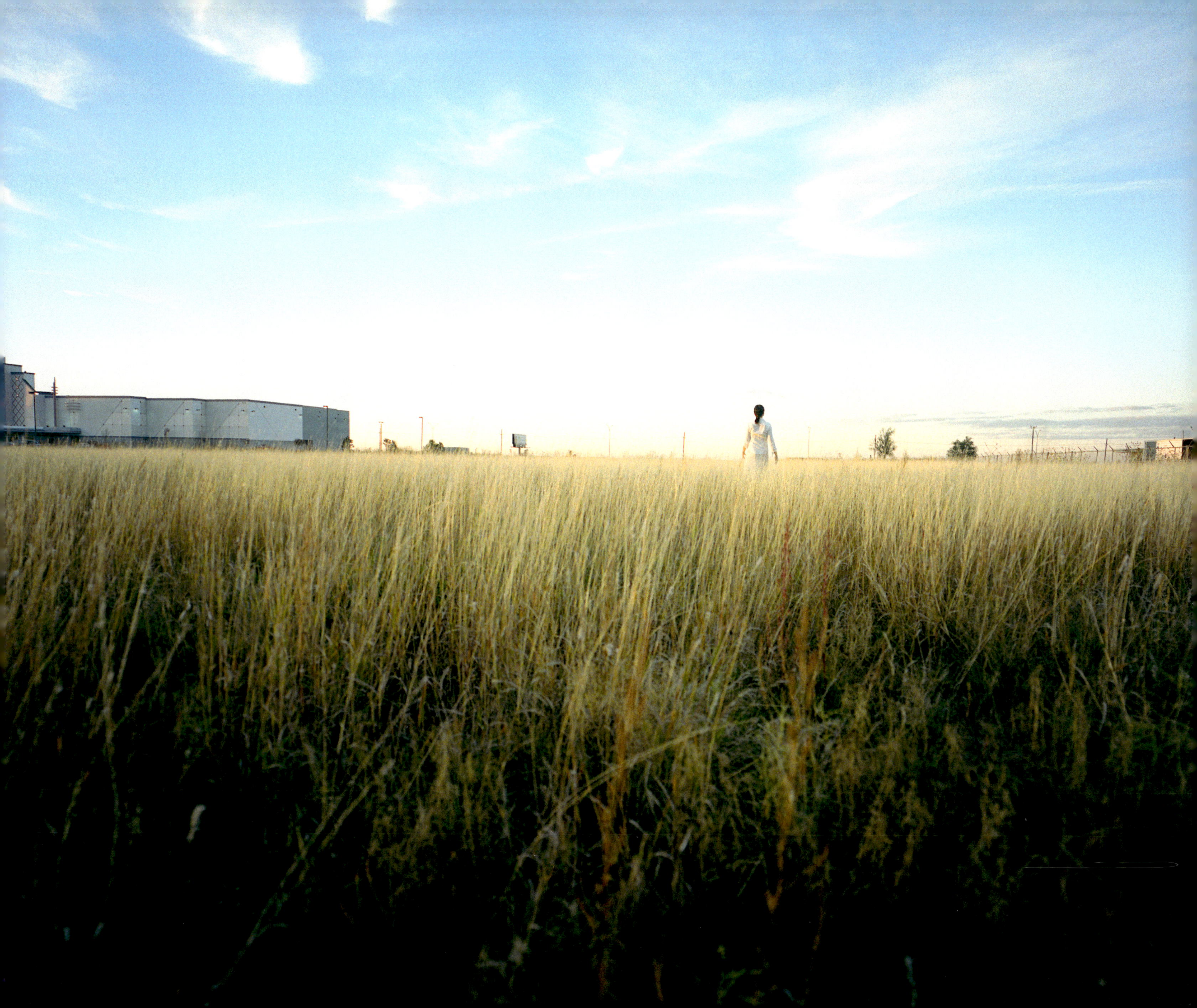

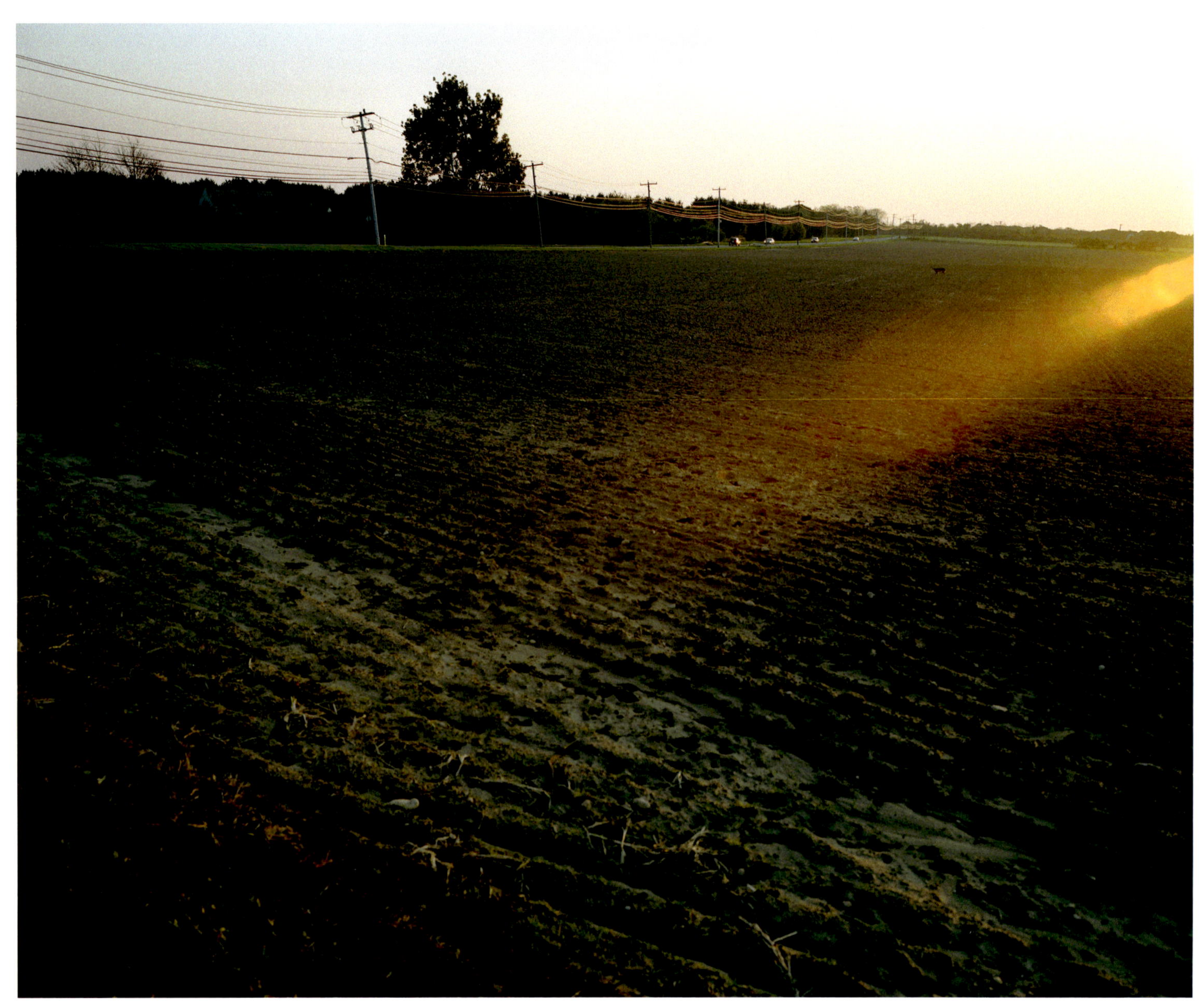

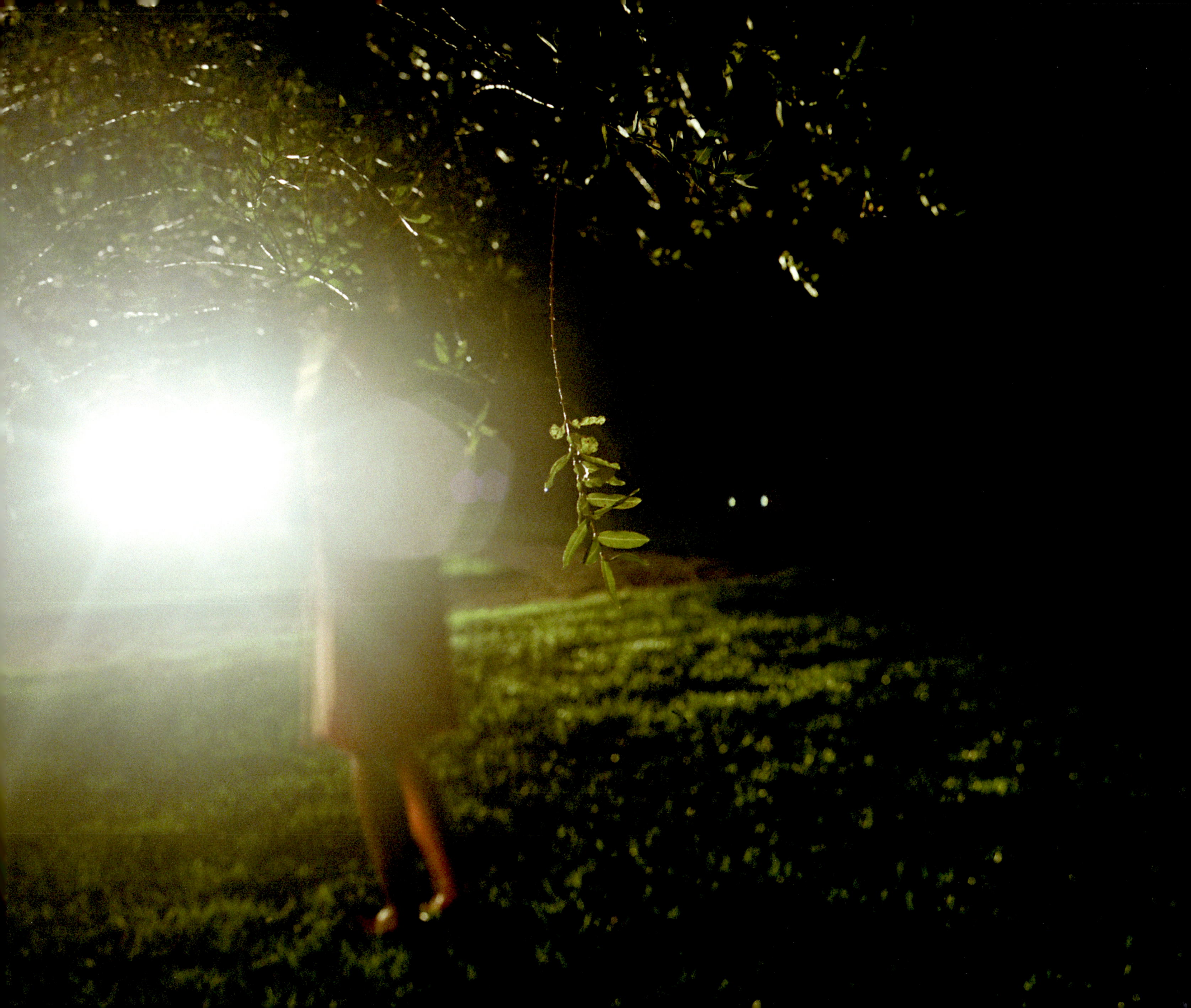

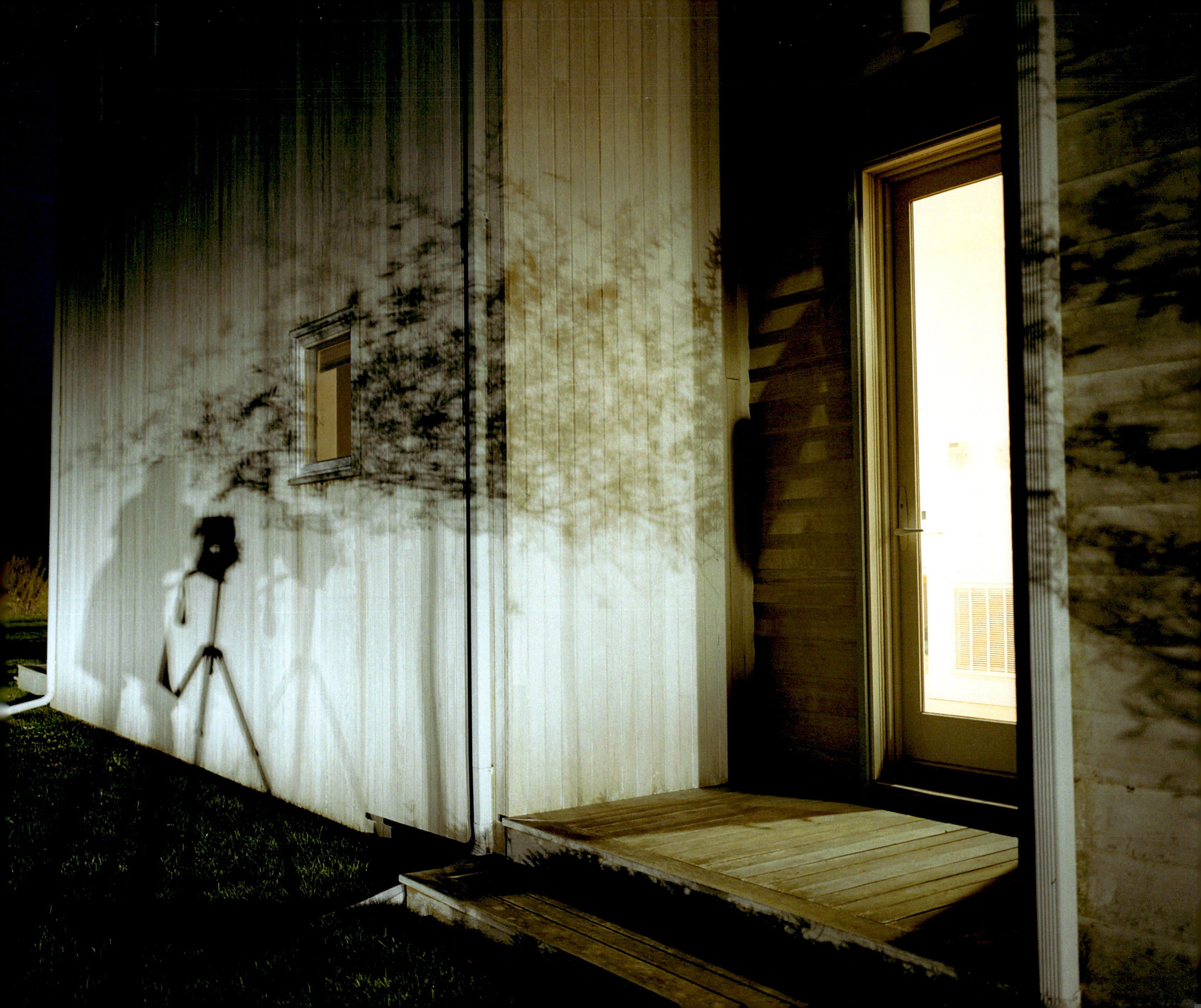

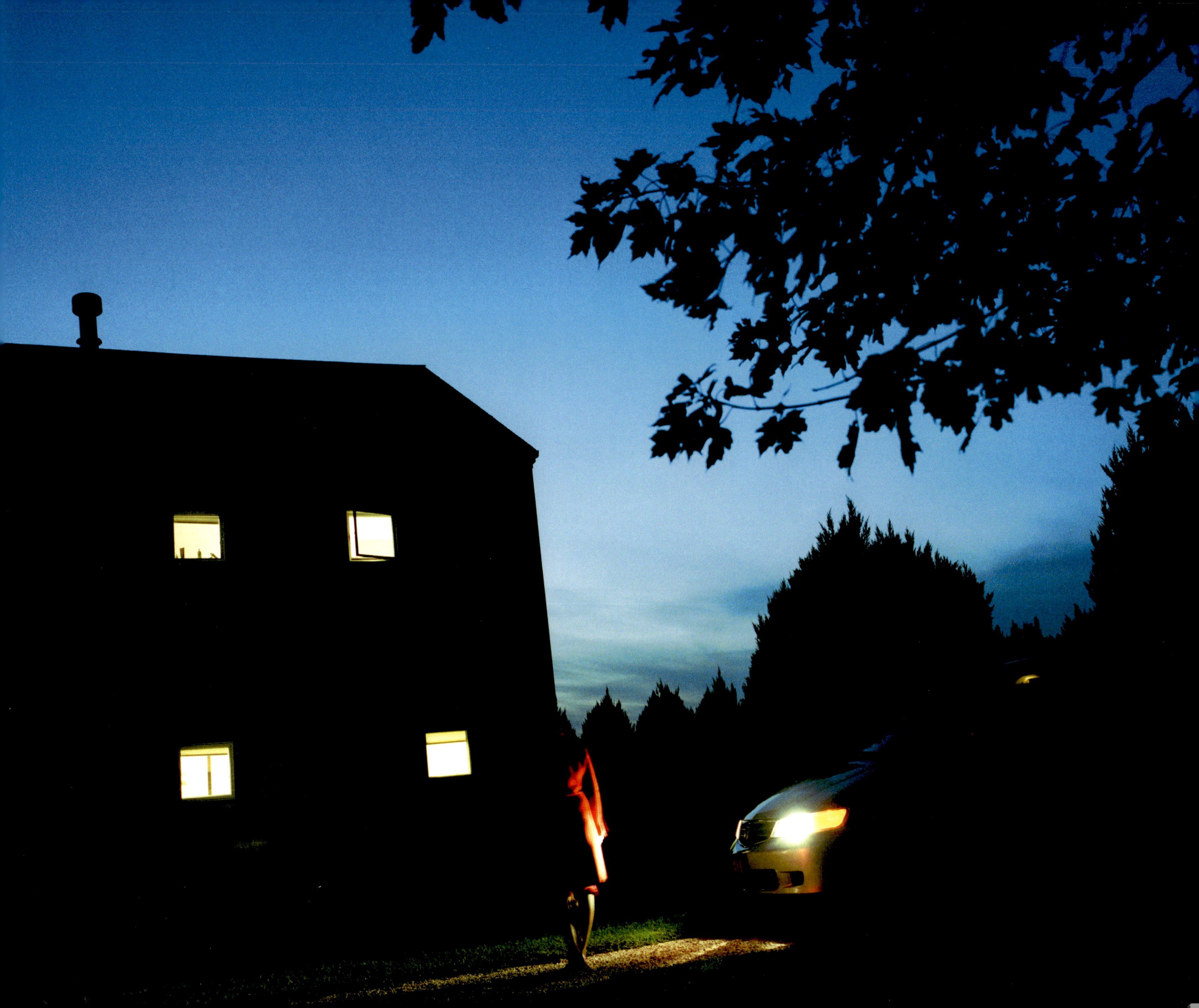

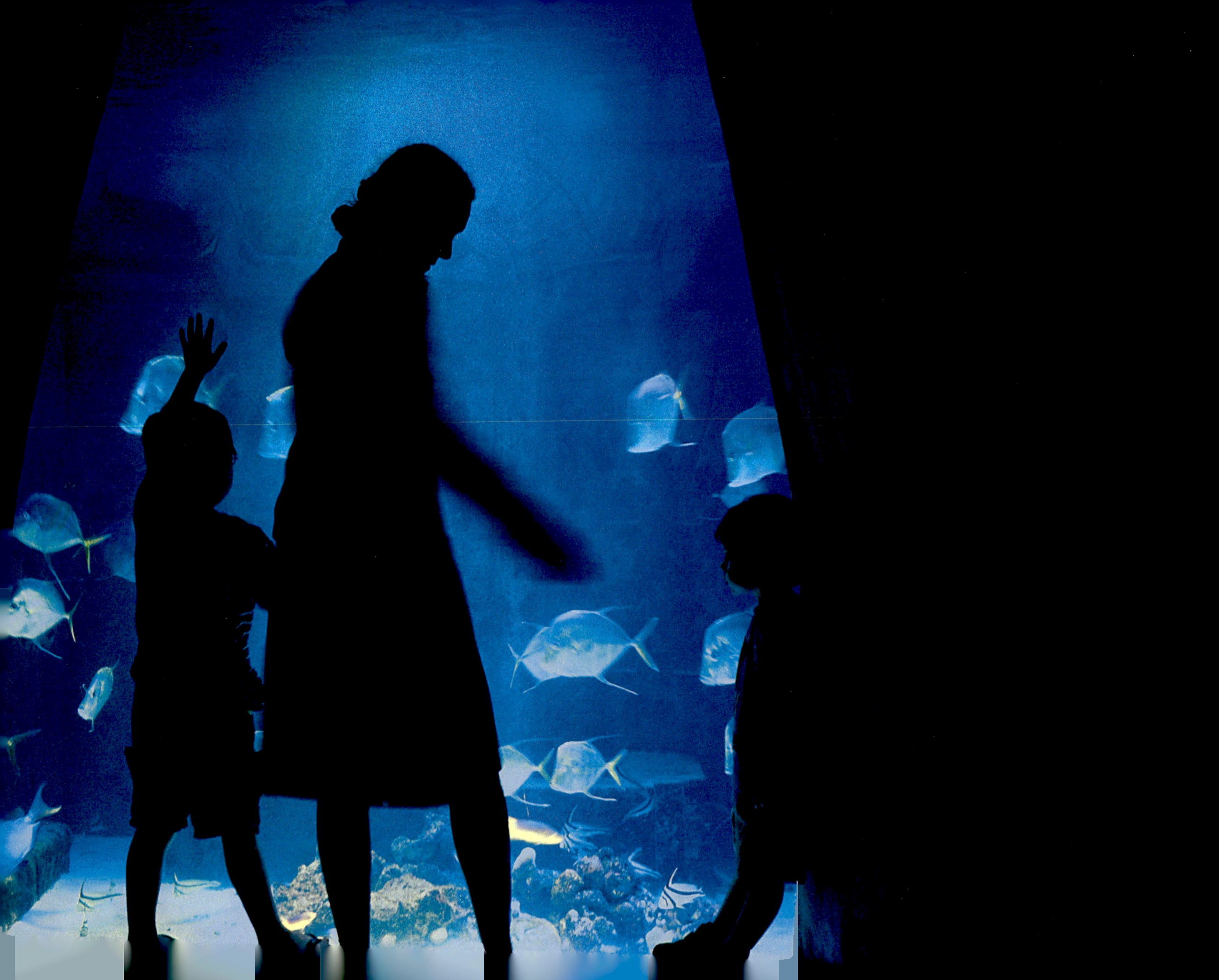

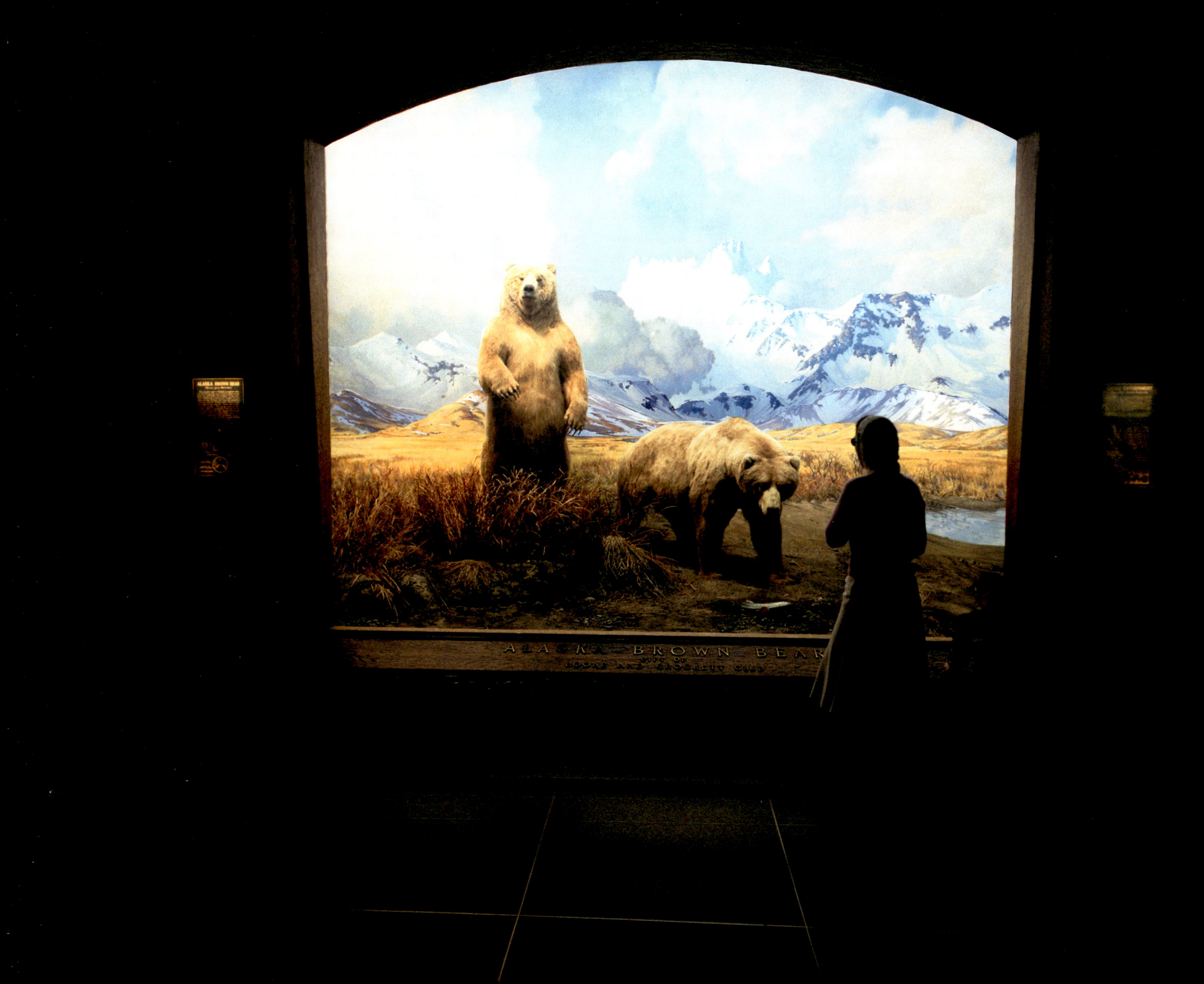

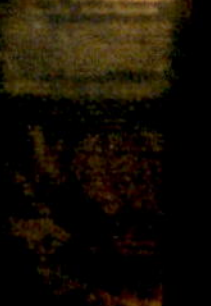
ALASKA BROWN BEAR

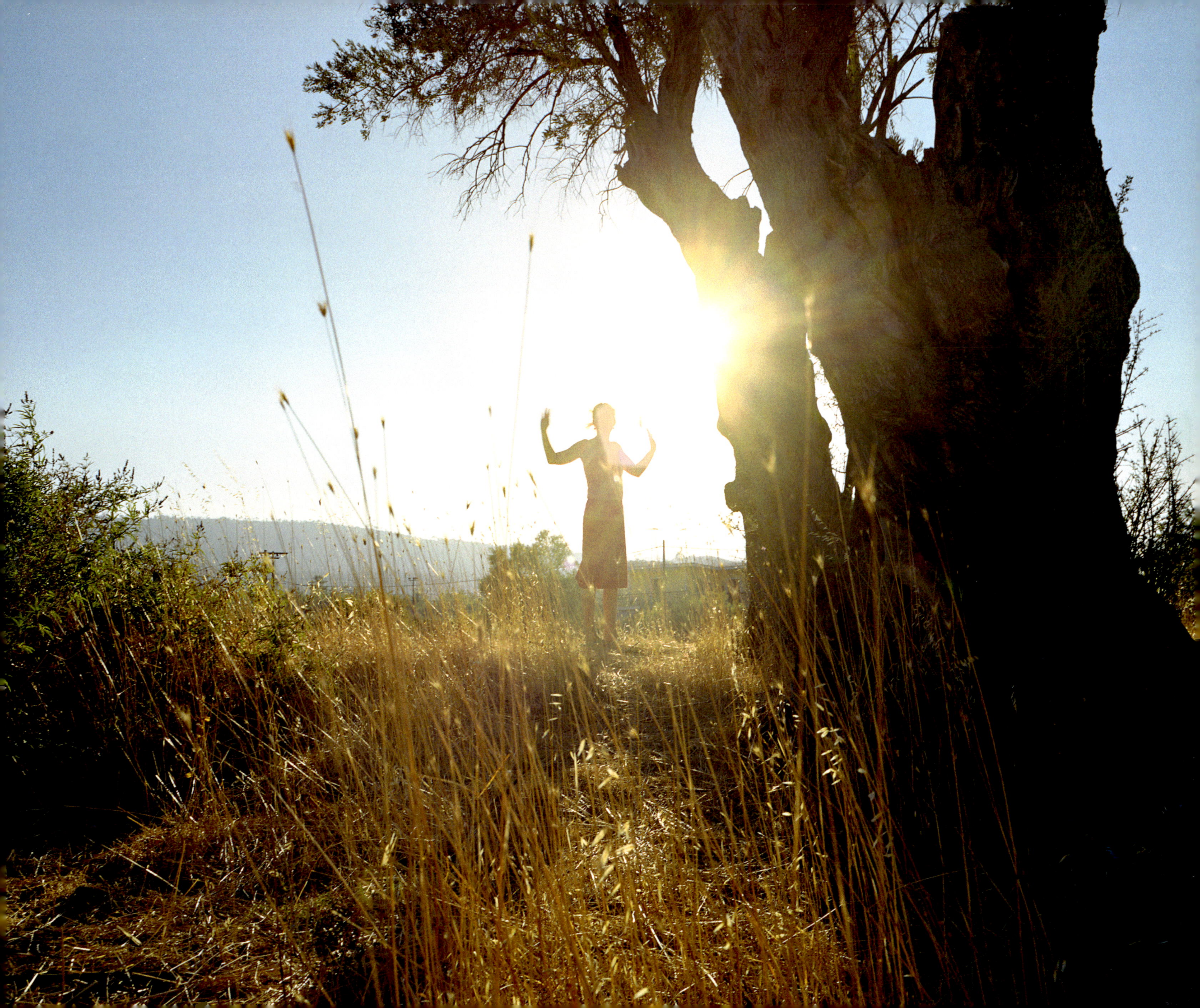

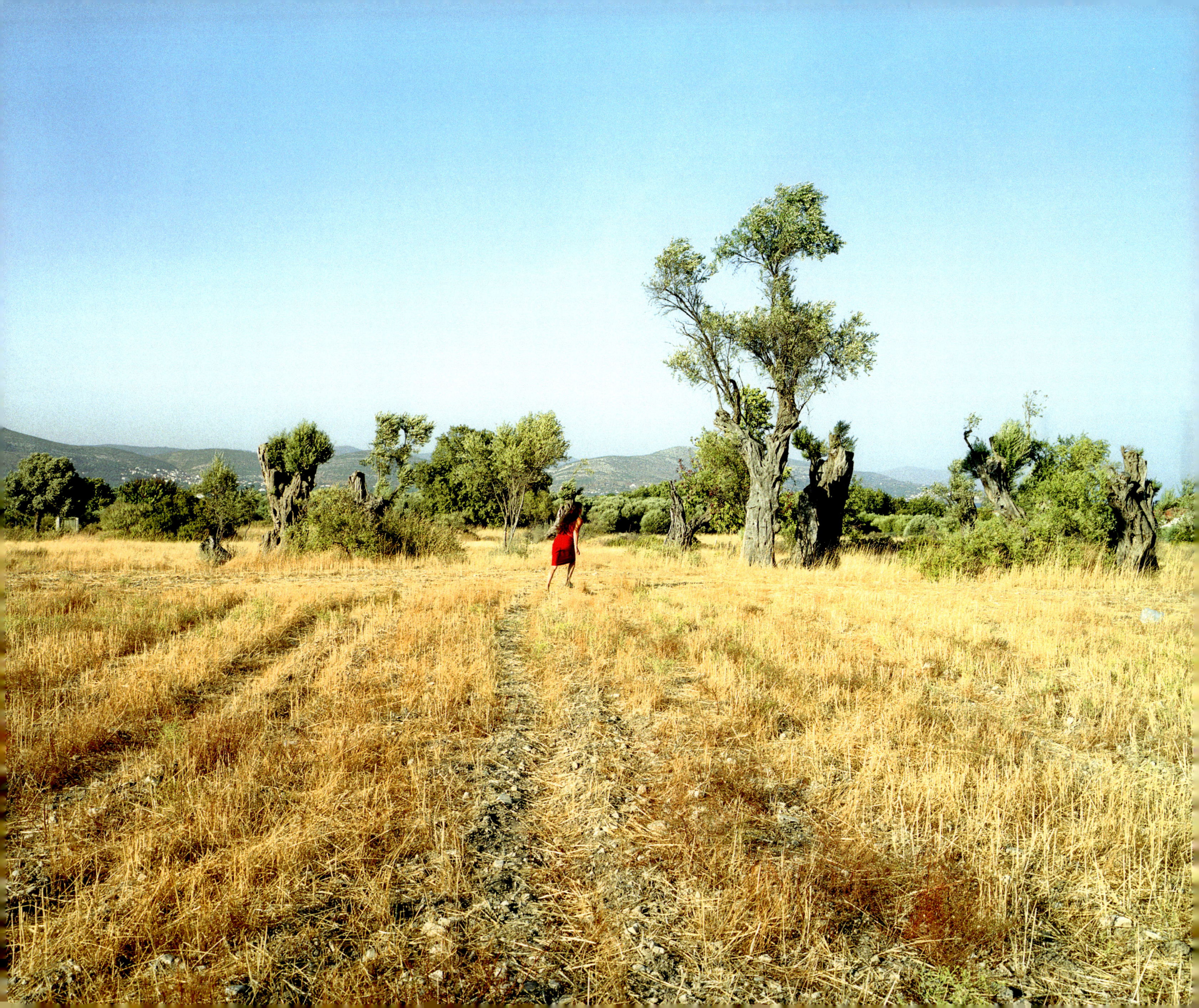

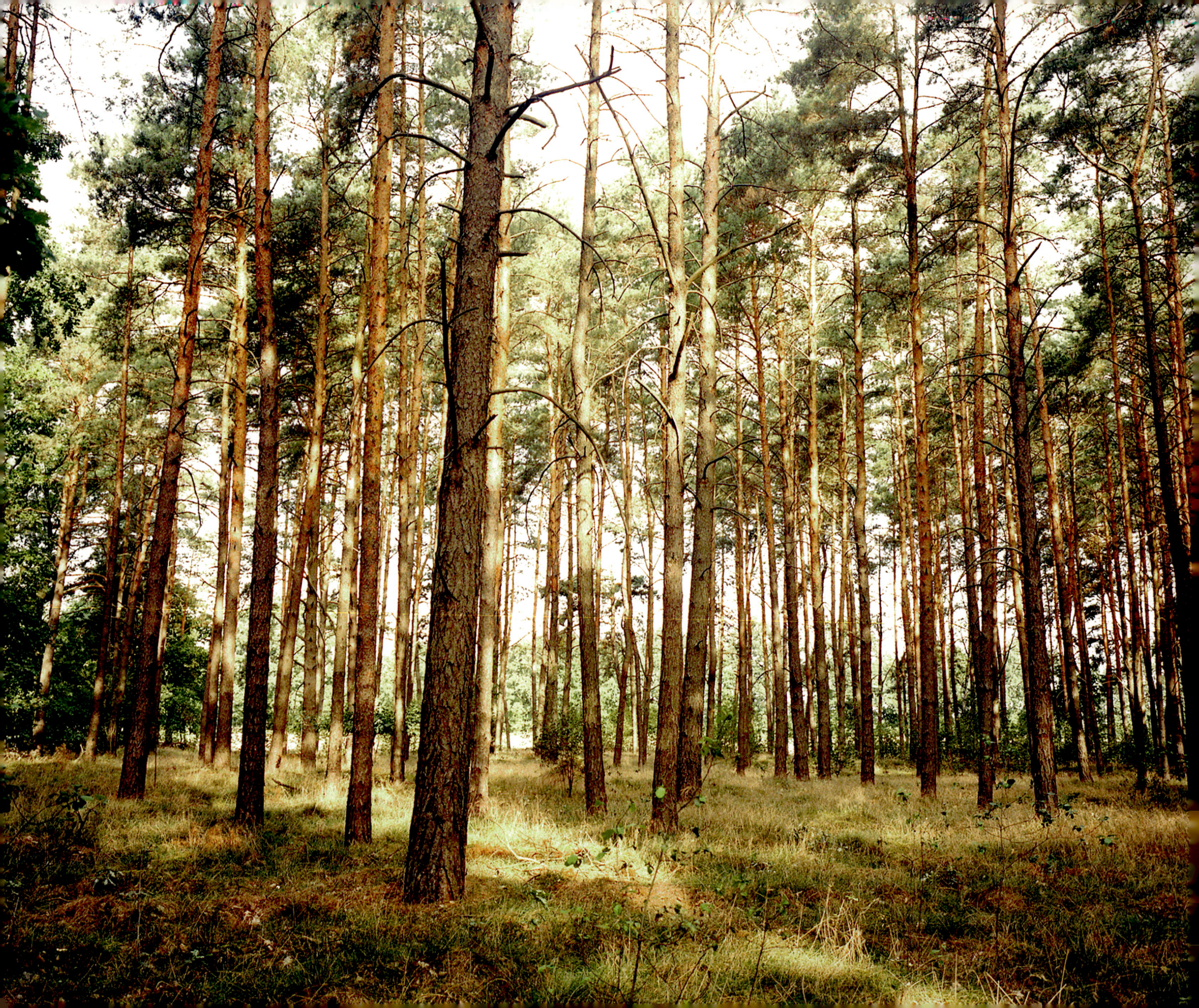

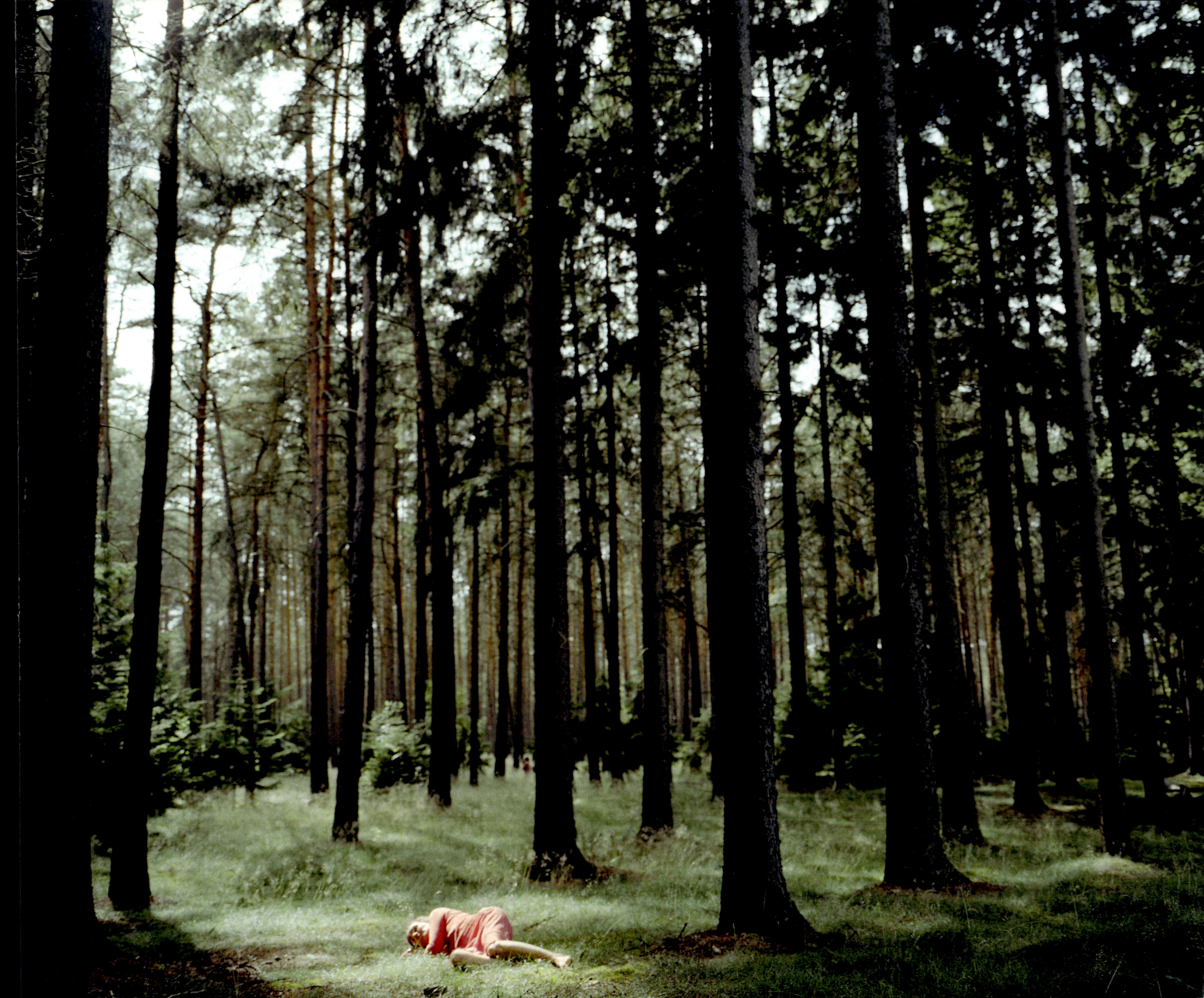

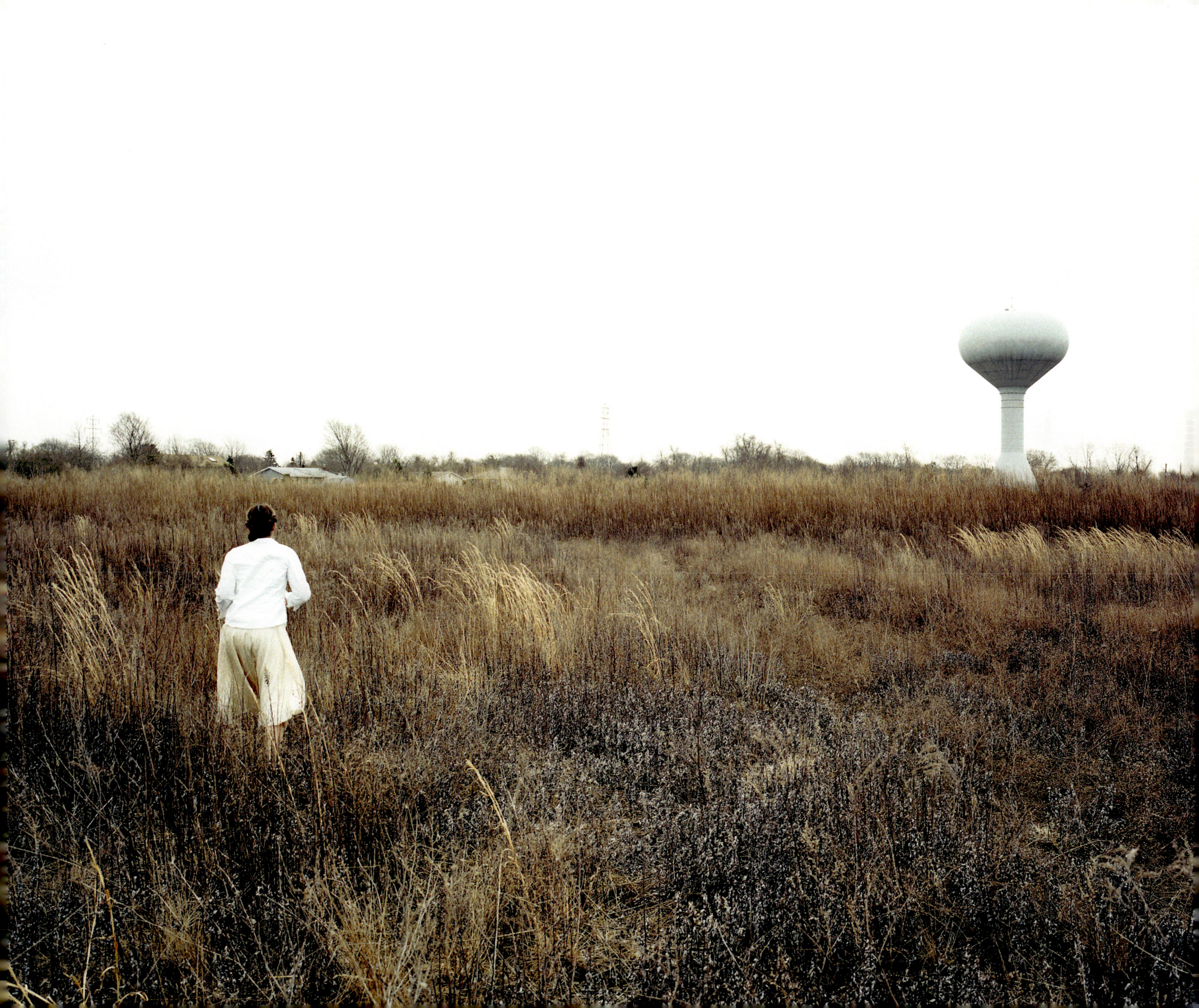

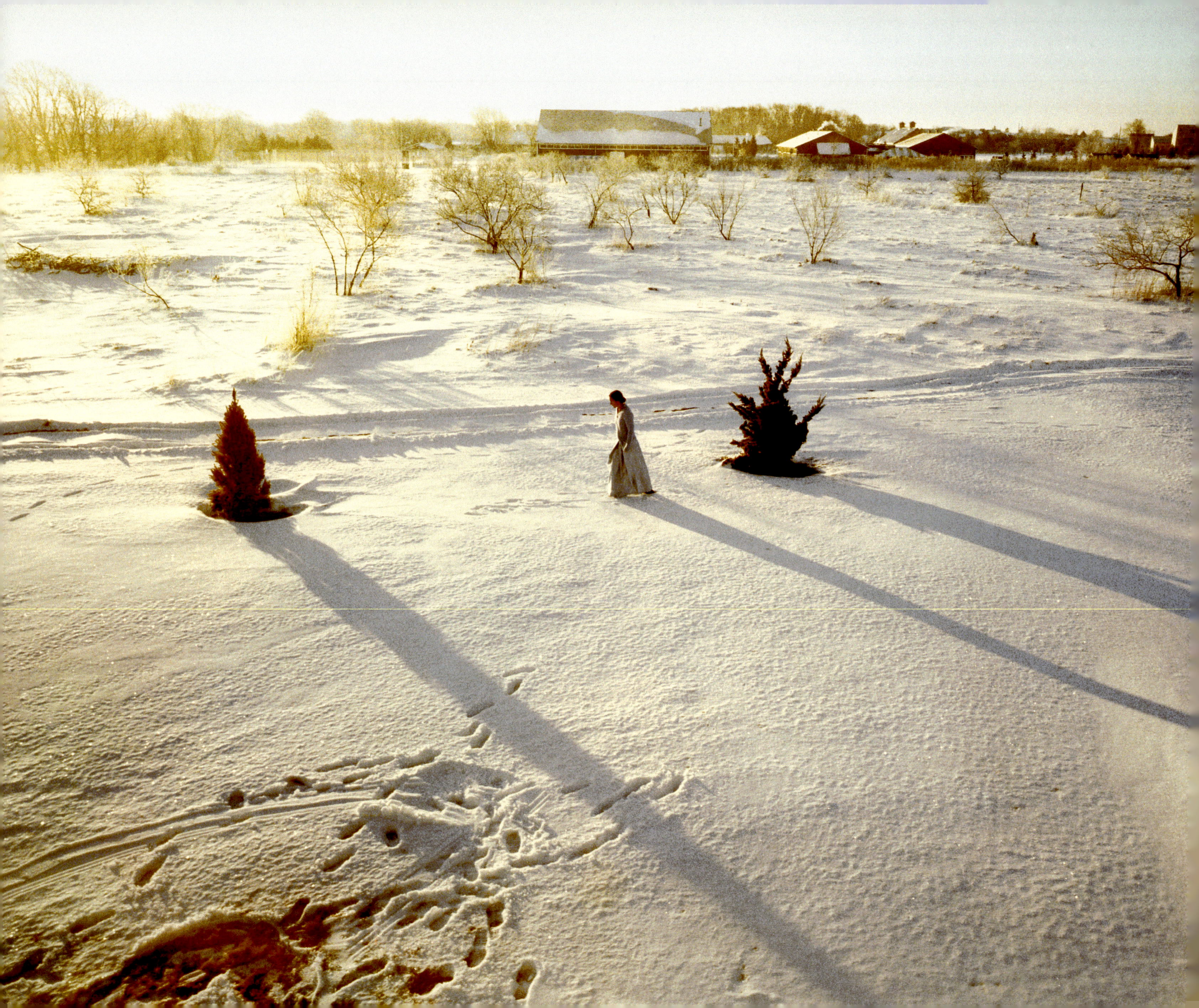

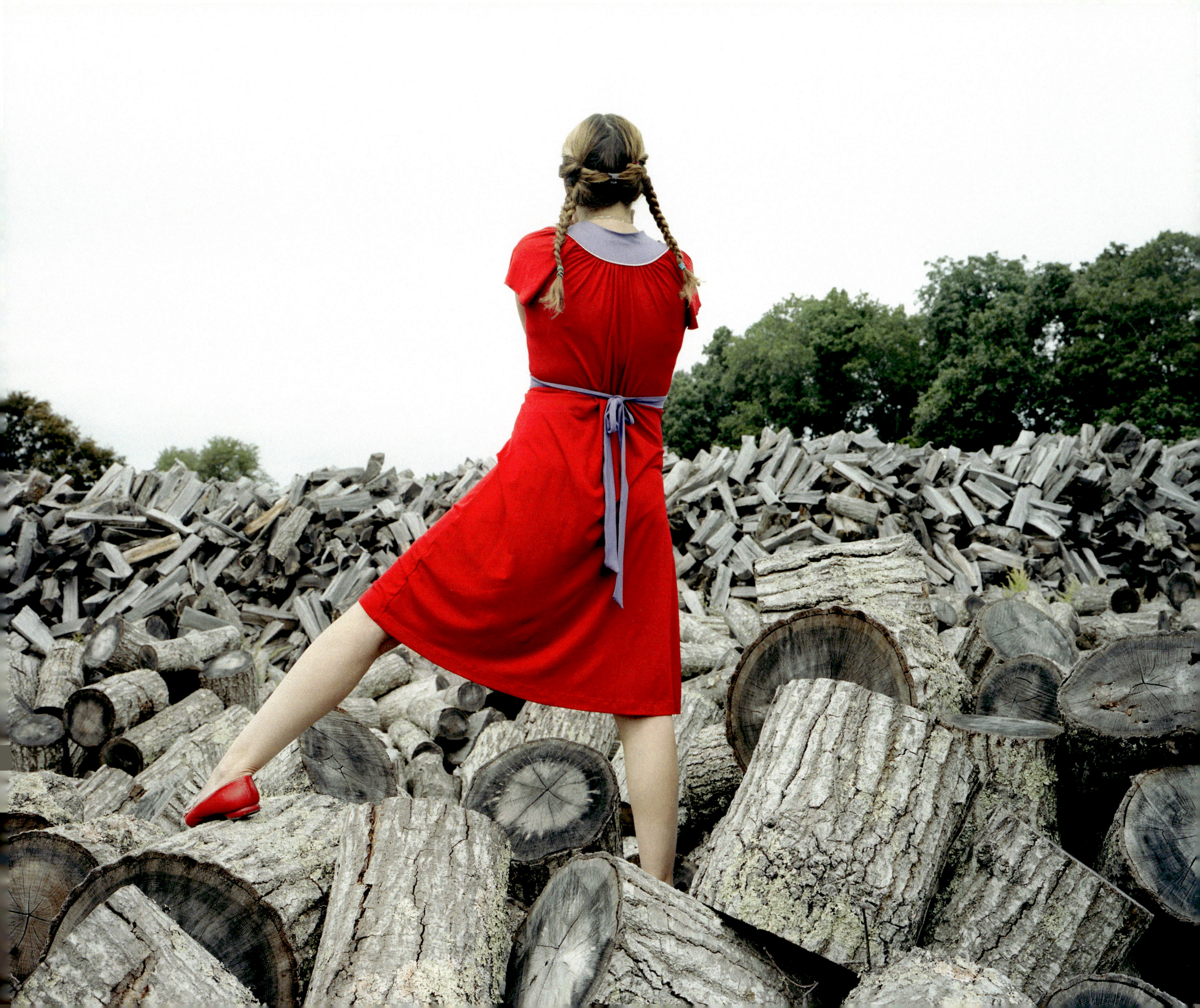

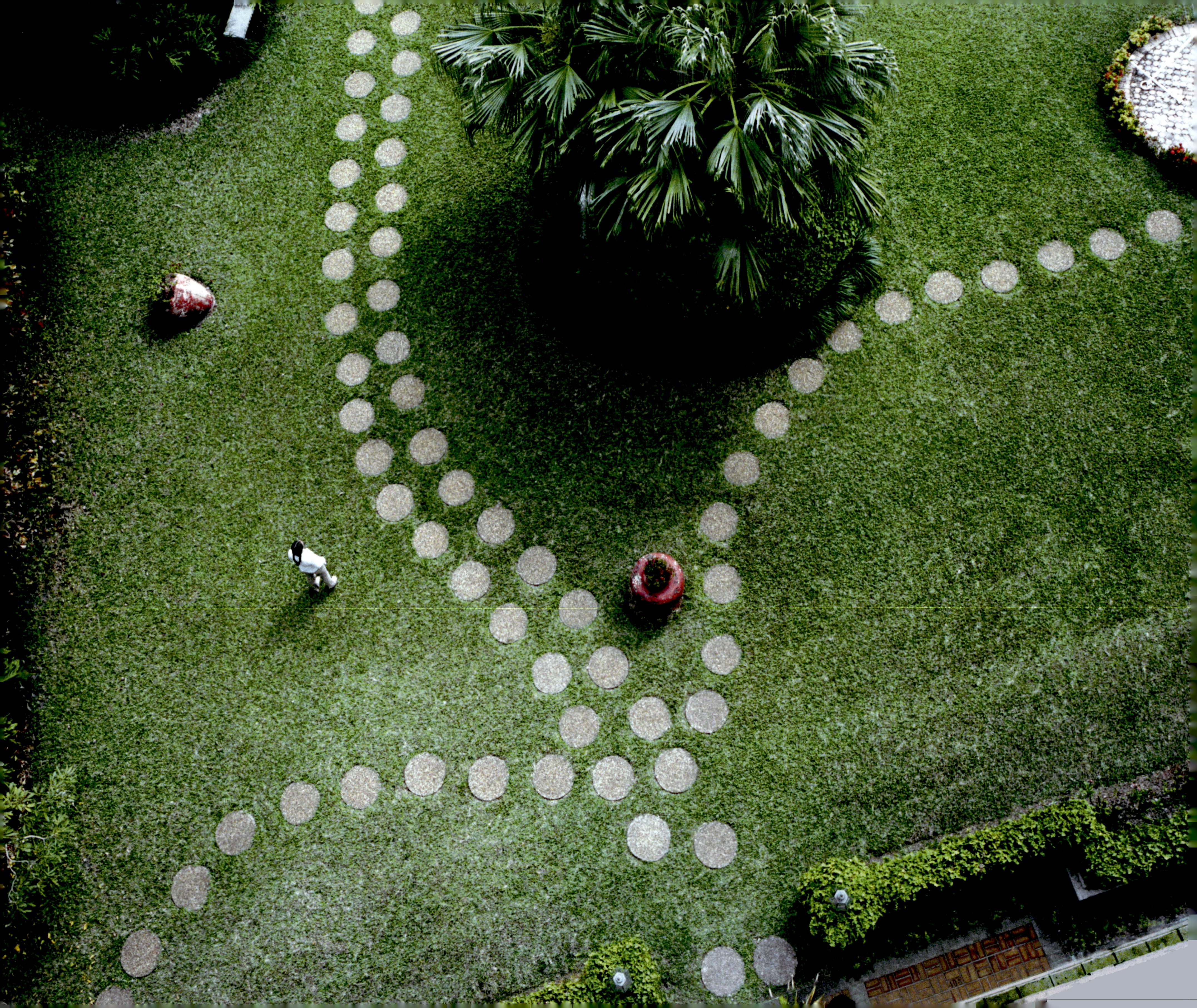

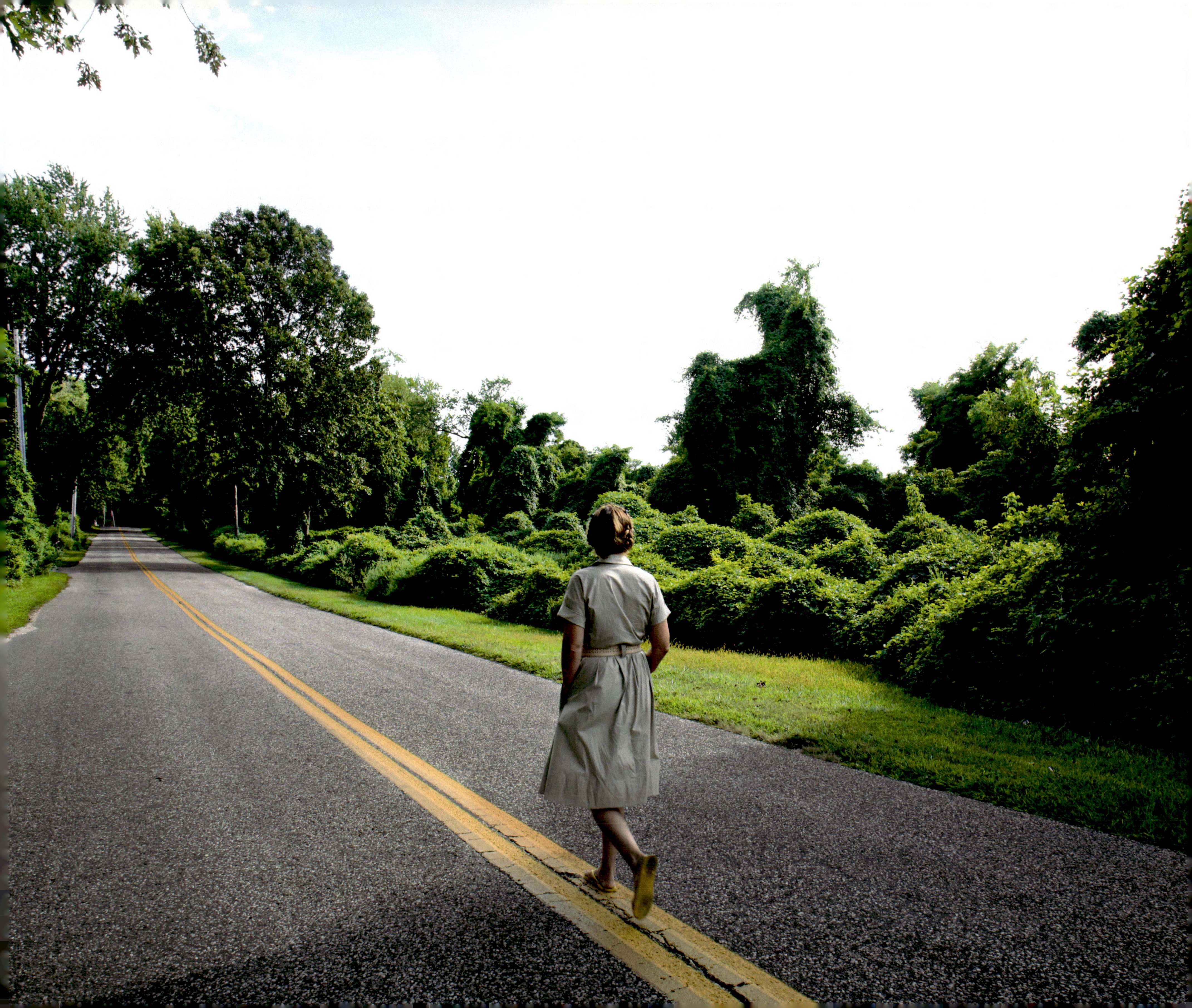

FILM STILLS

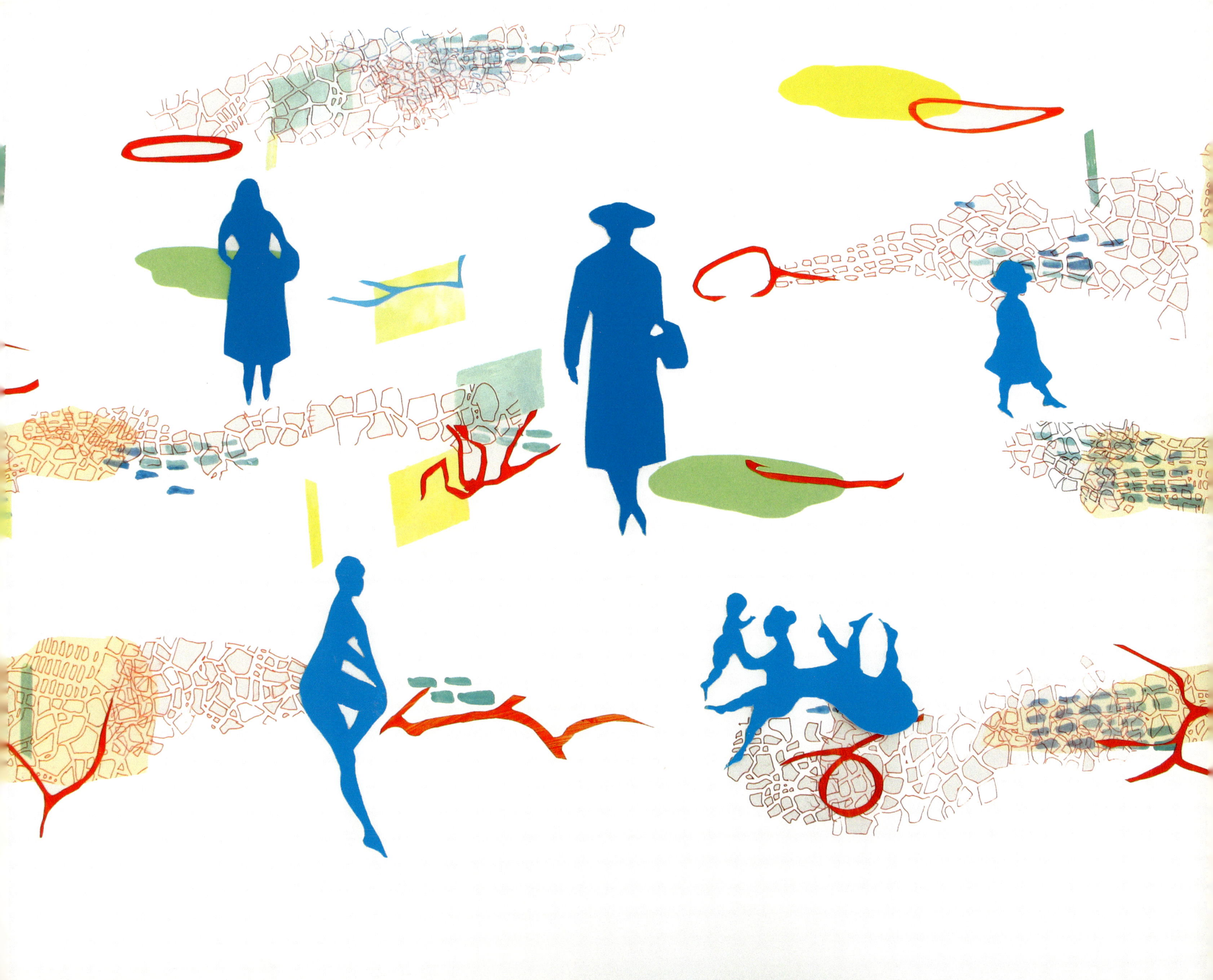

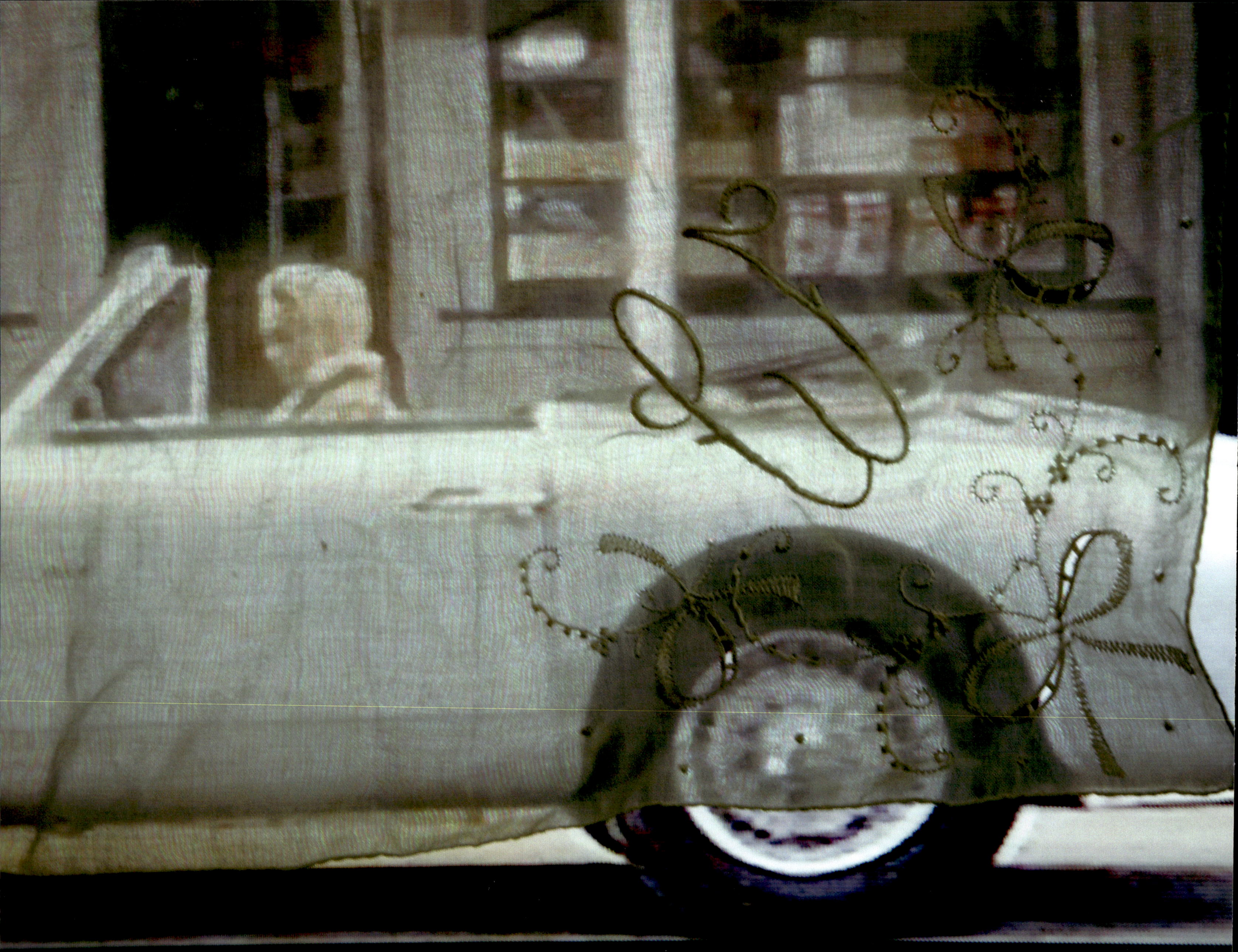

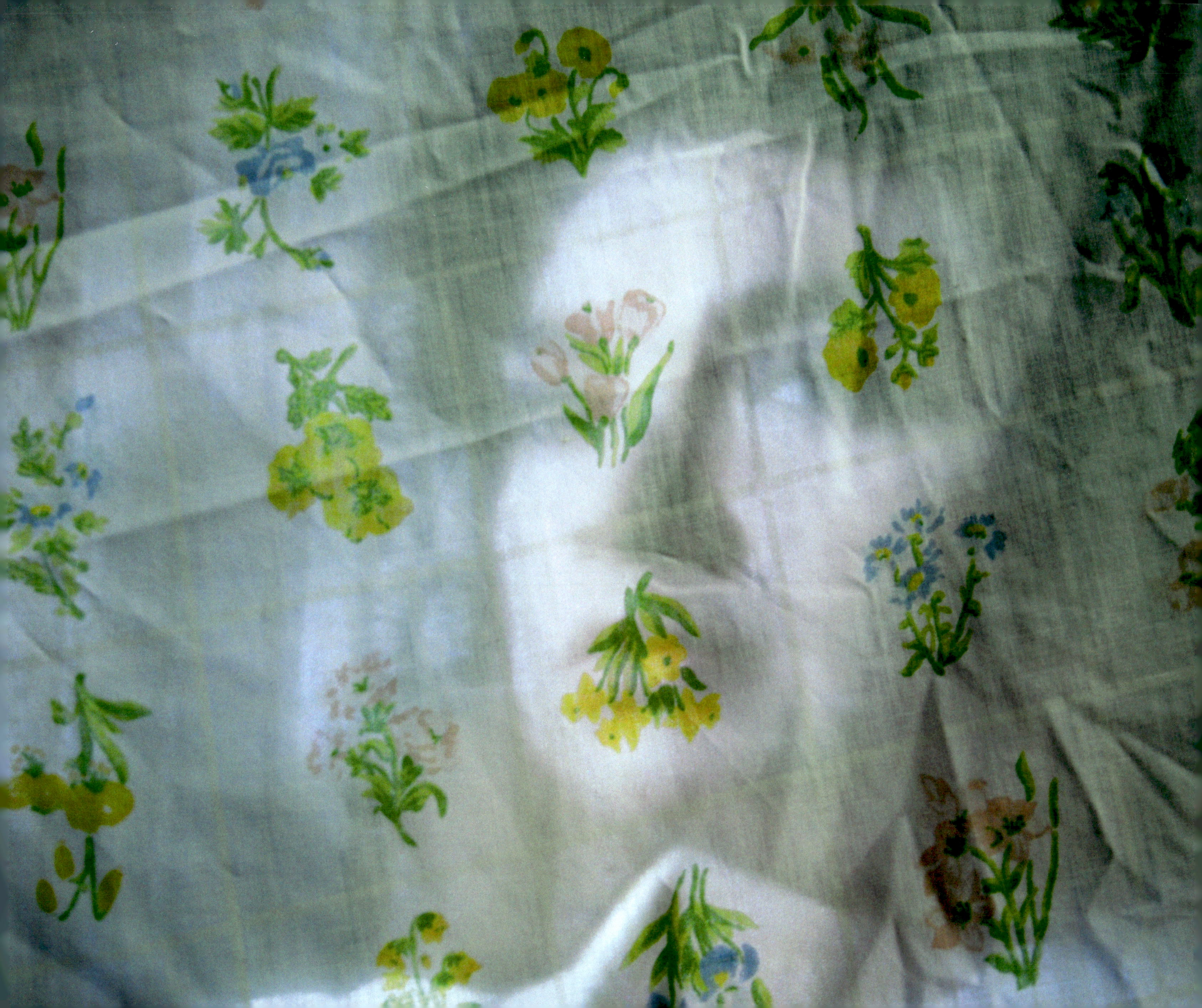

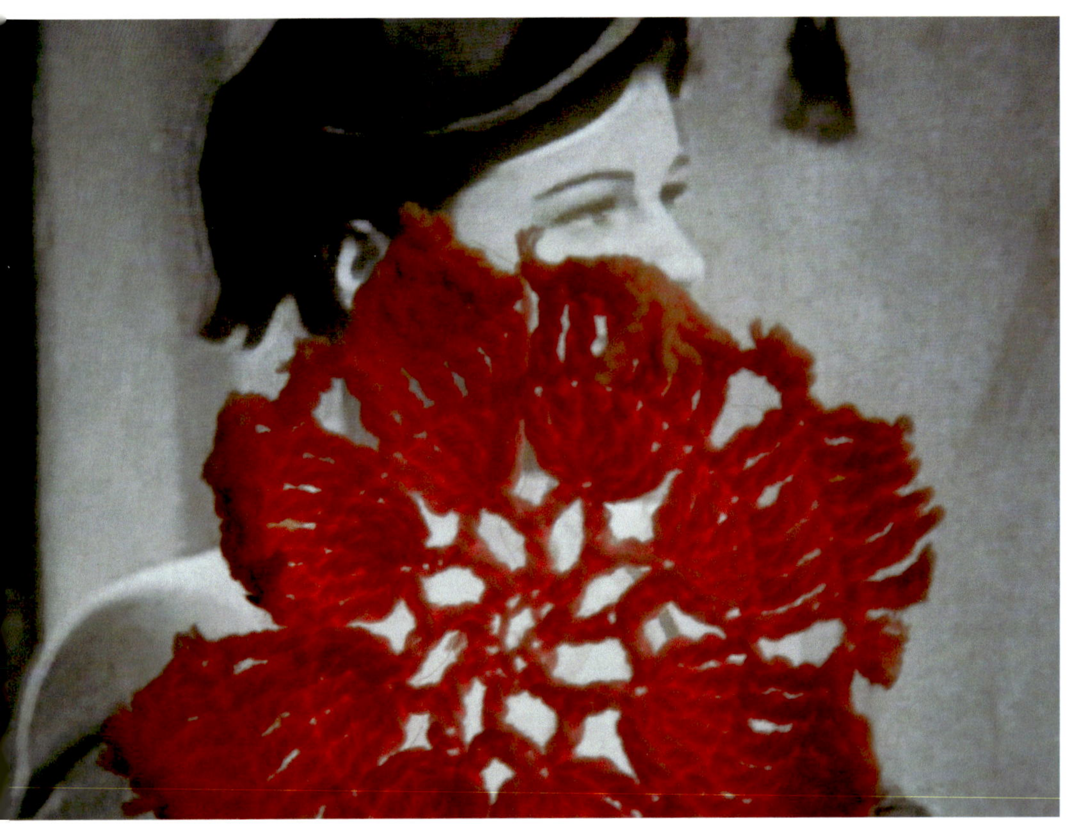

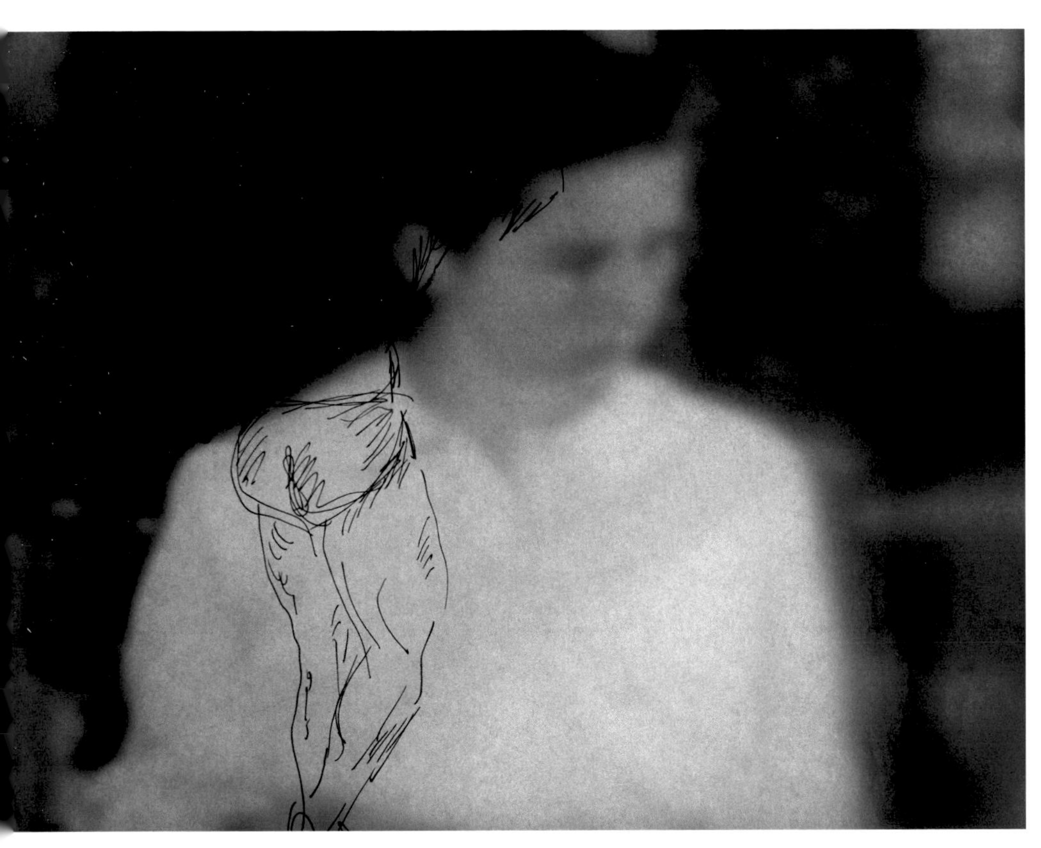

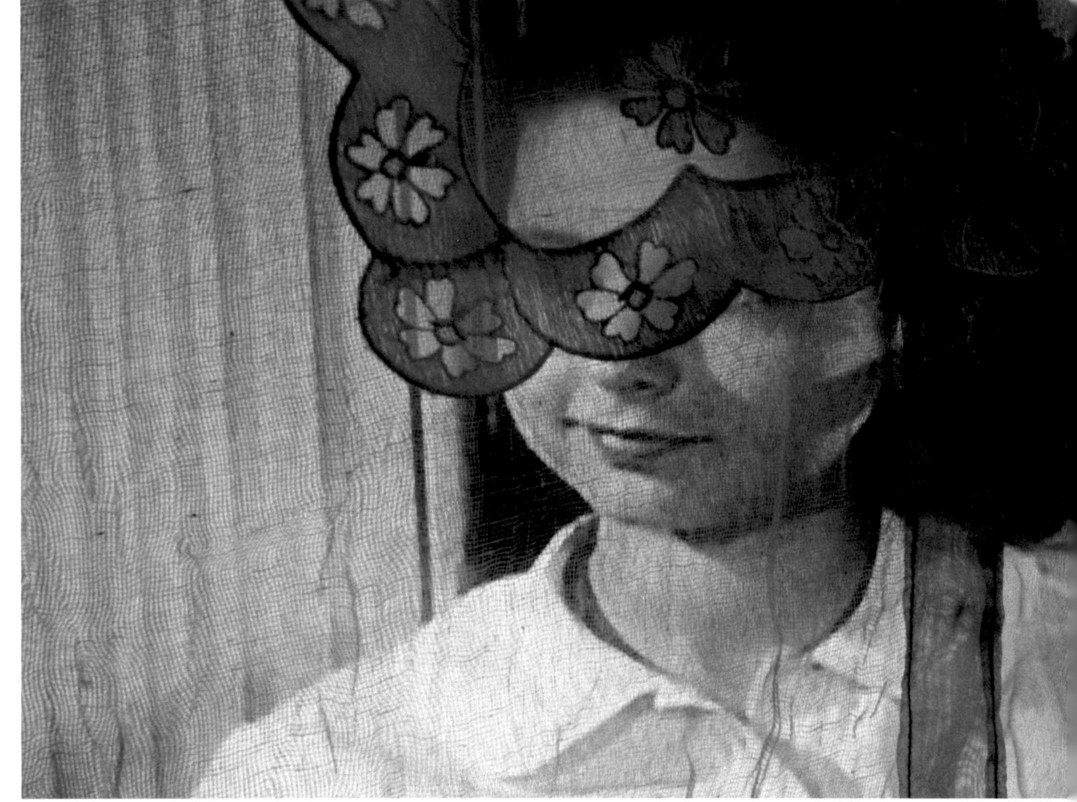

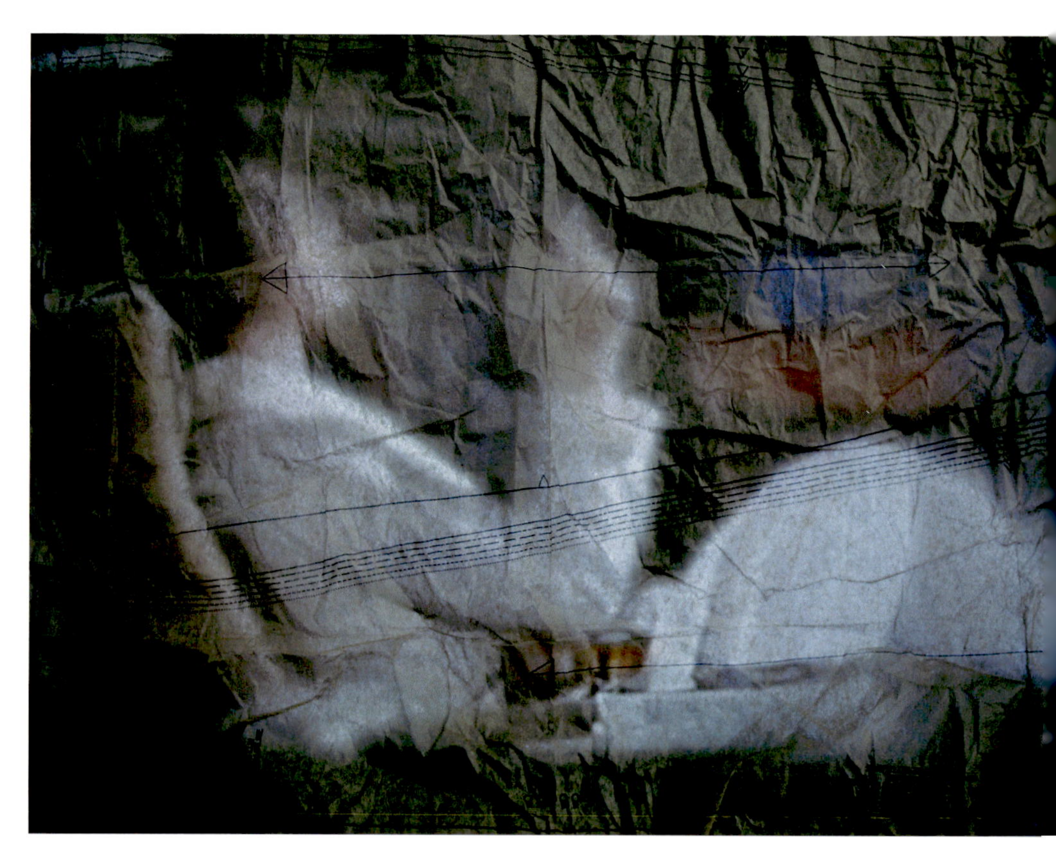

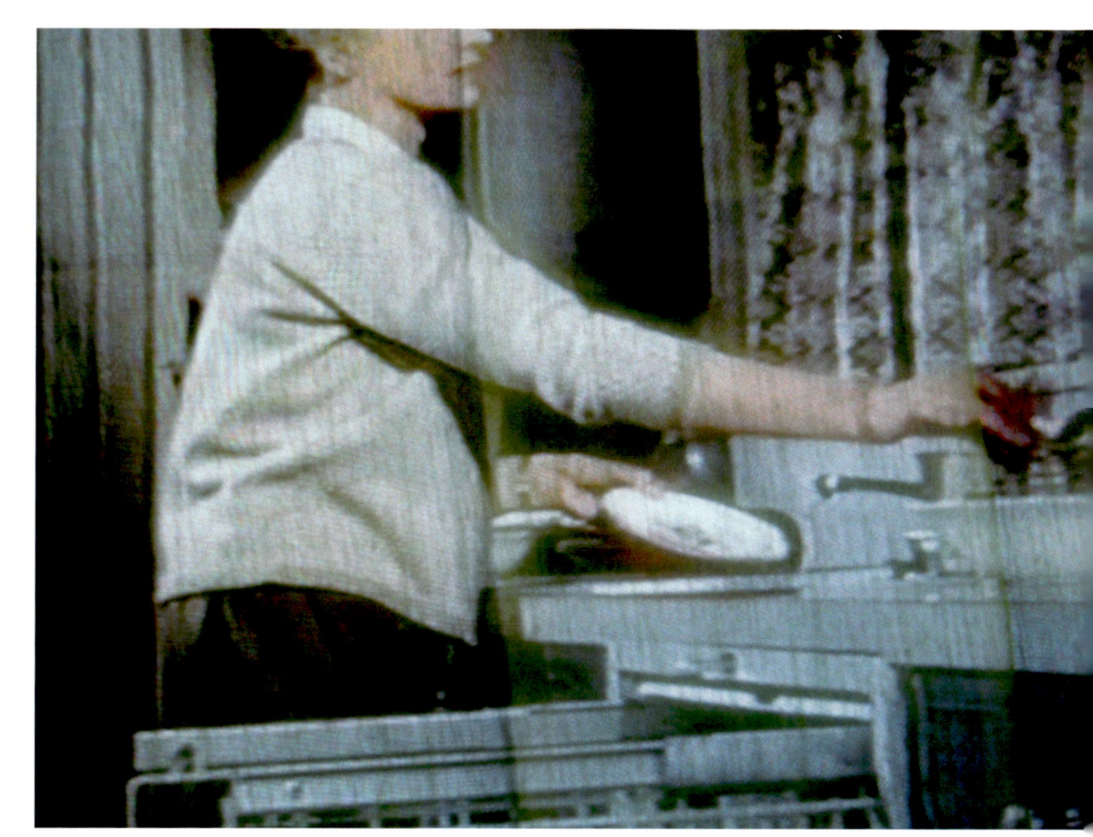

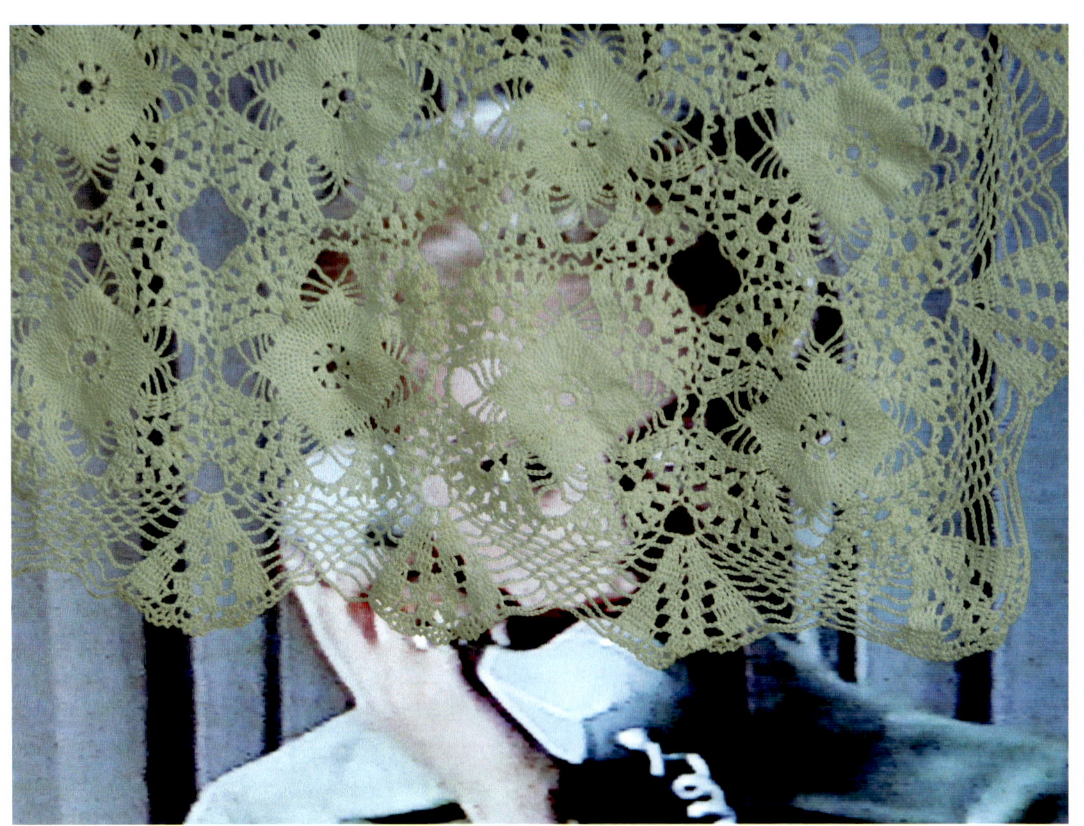

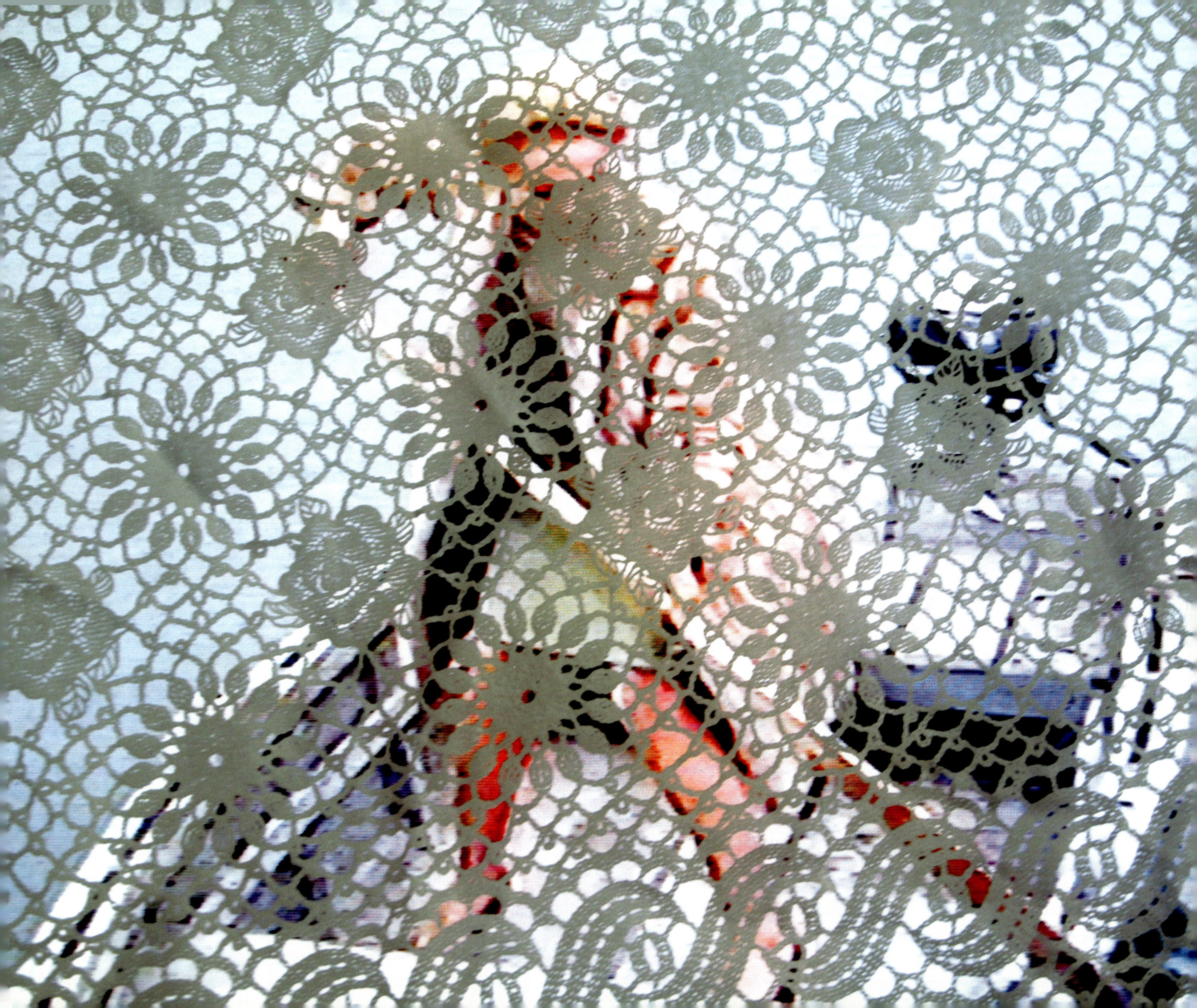

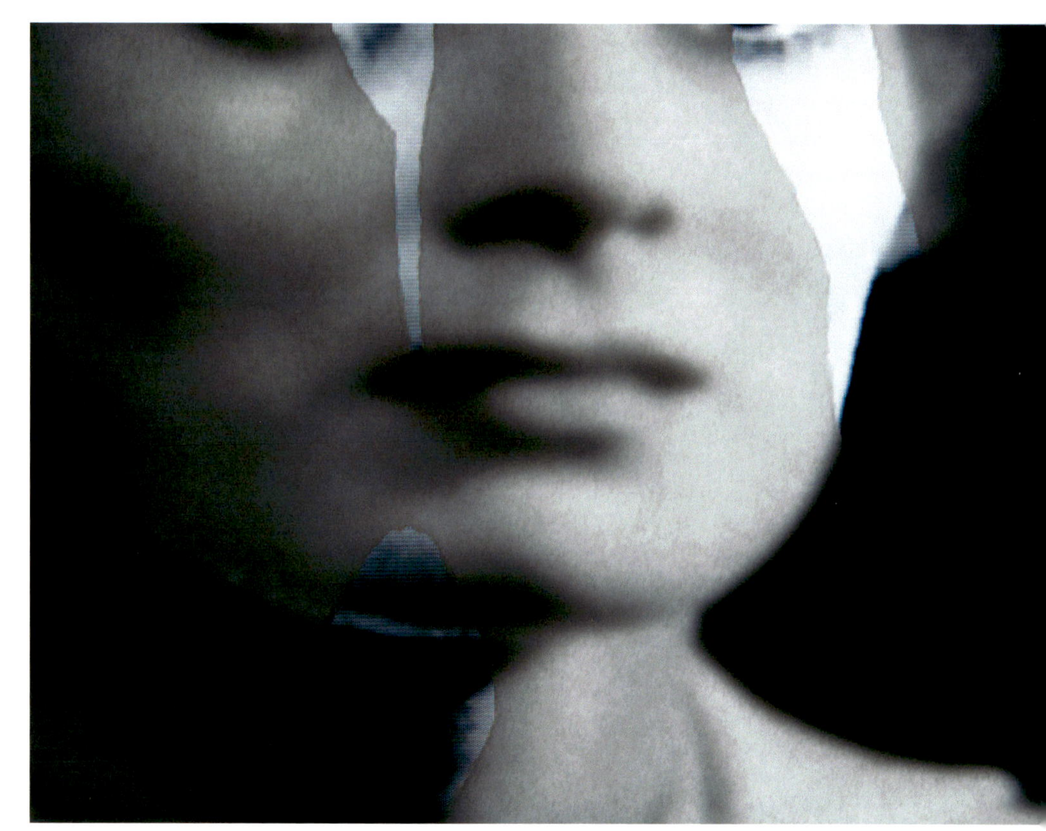

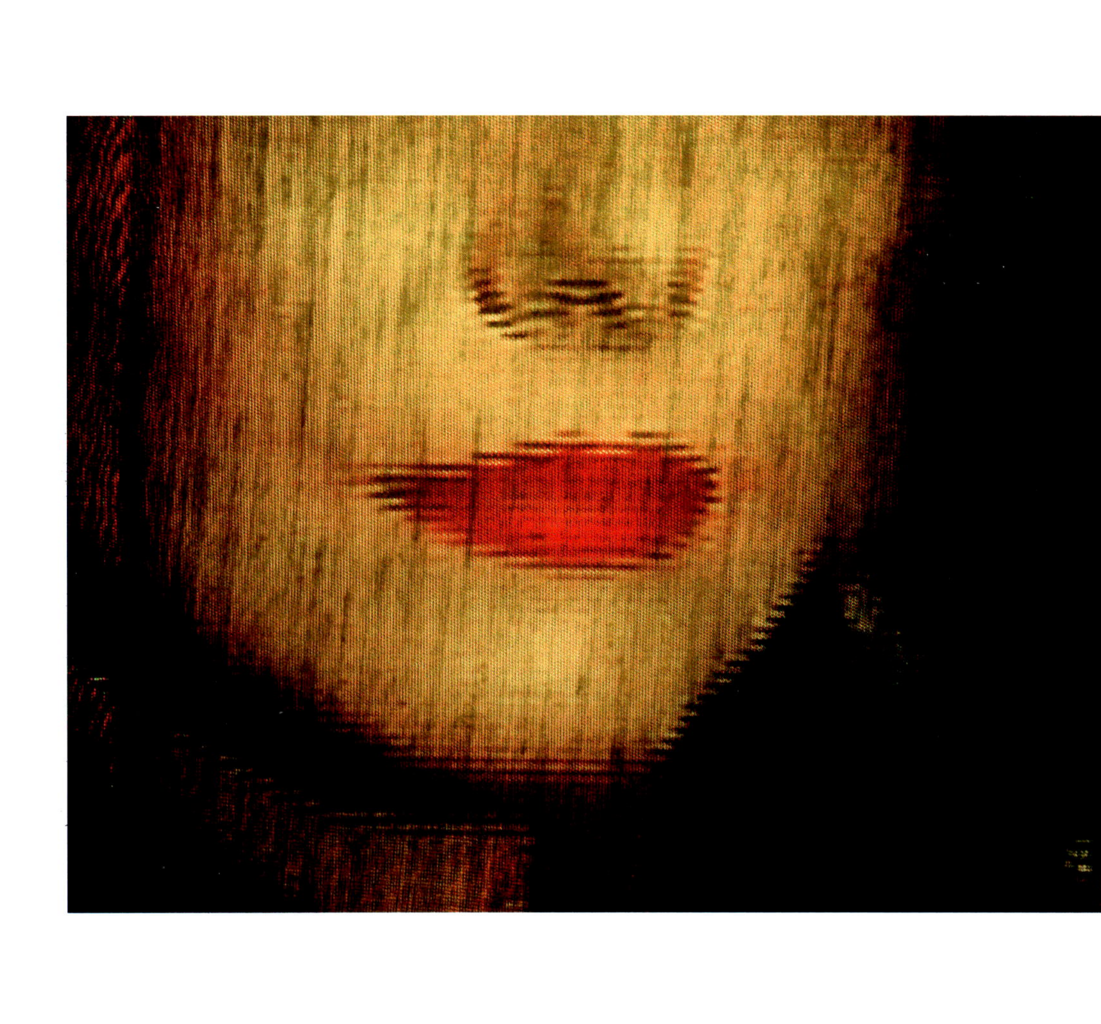

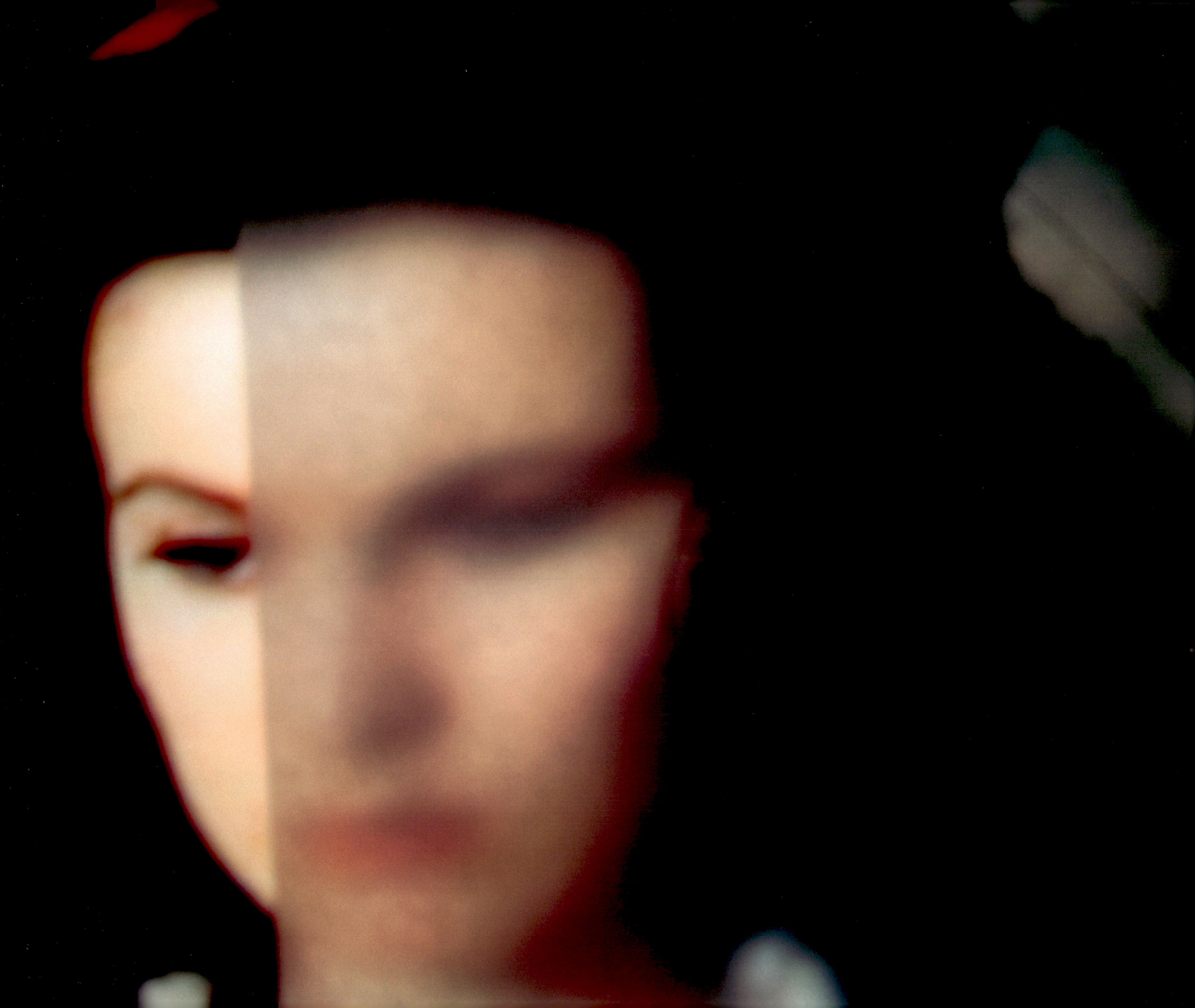

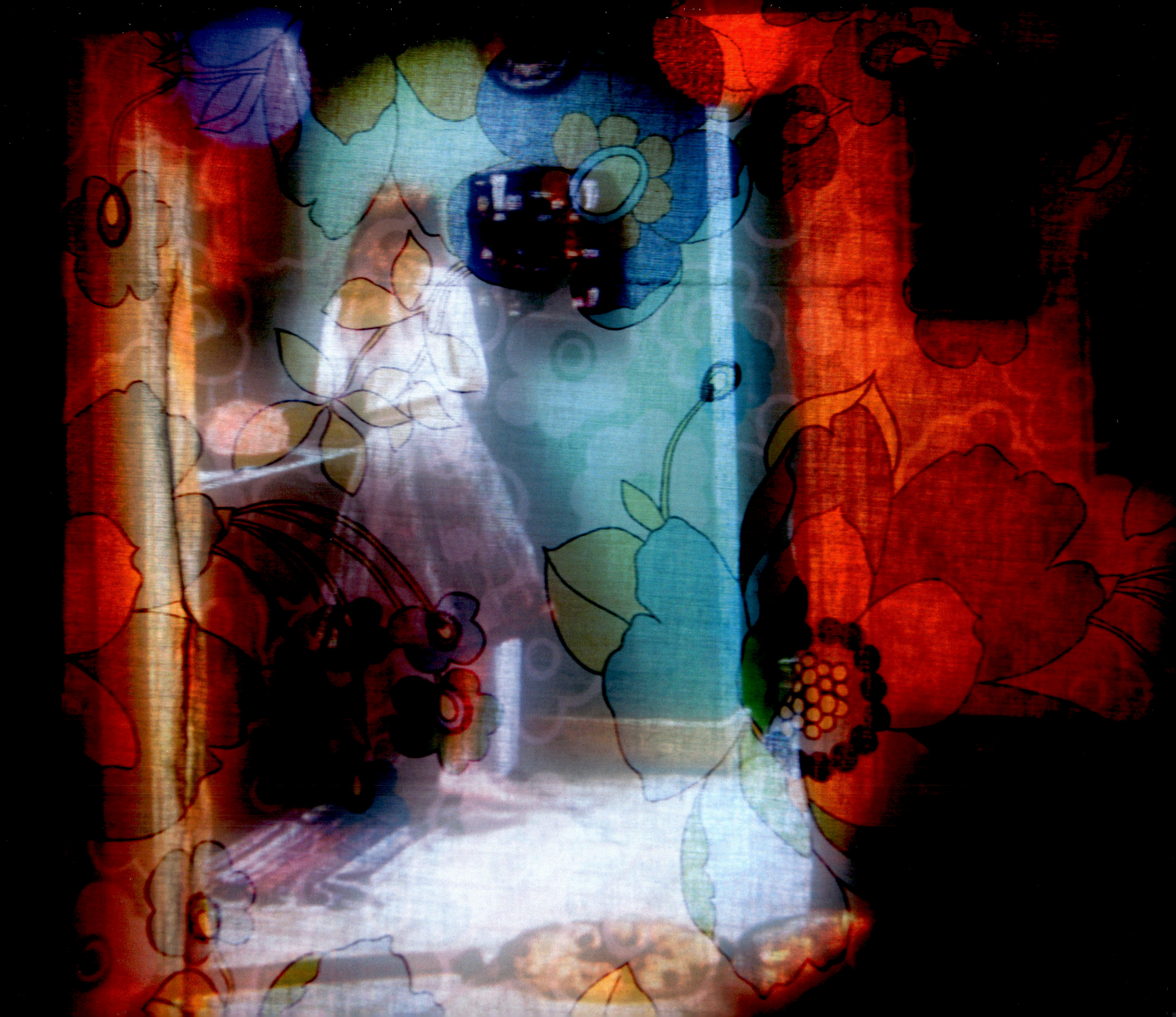

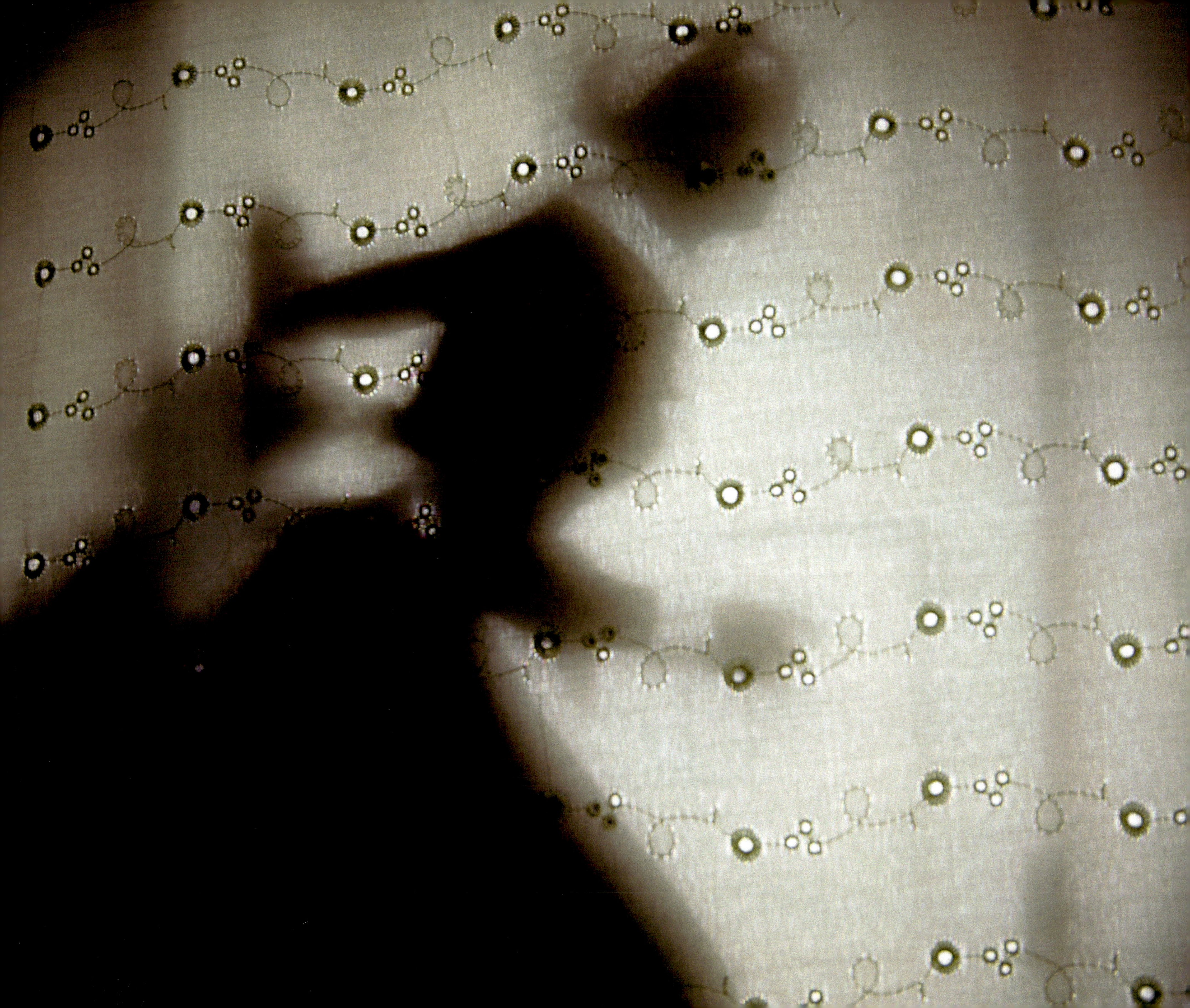

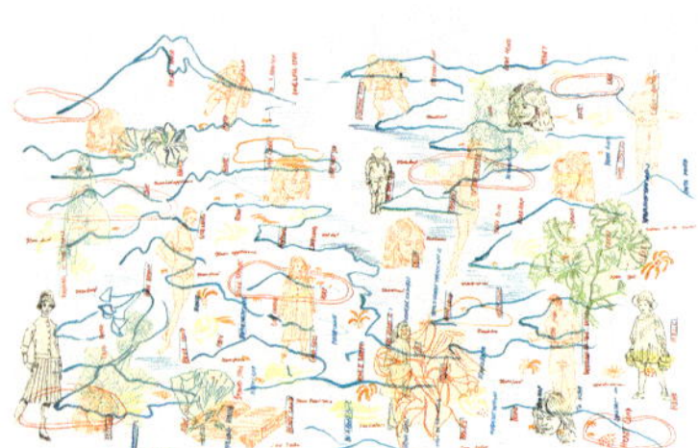
Women in Hokusai's Map
Mixed media on paper, 30 x 40 inches,
2006

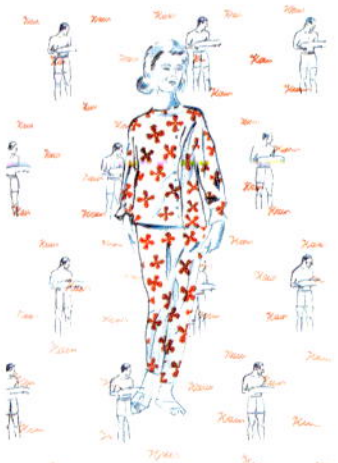
Woman with Housedress
Mixed media on paper, 30 x 40 inches,
2004

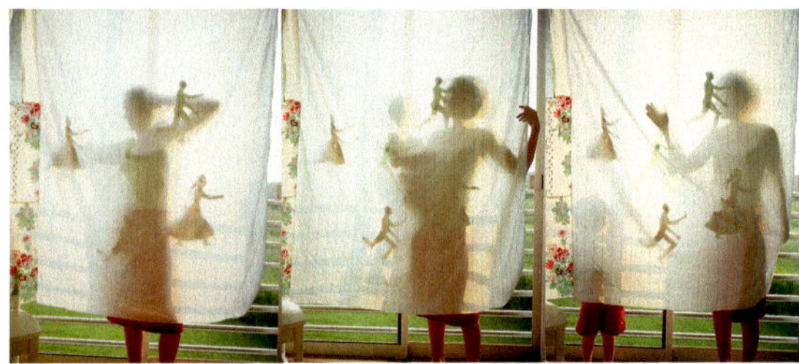
Three Silhouettes
Bridgehampton, 2003

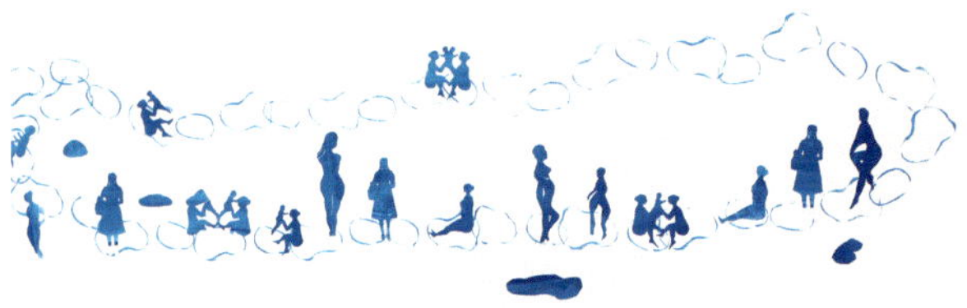
Blue Cycle of a Woman's Life
Mixed Media, Cut out Painted Paper, 48 x 96 inches,
2008

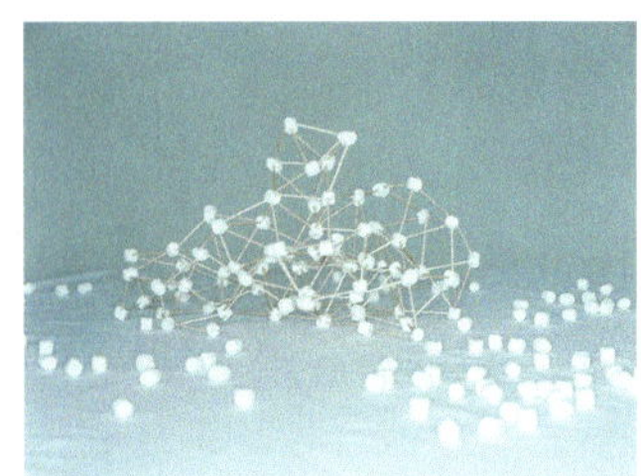
Marshmallow DNA Model
Bridgehampton, 2003

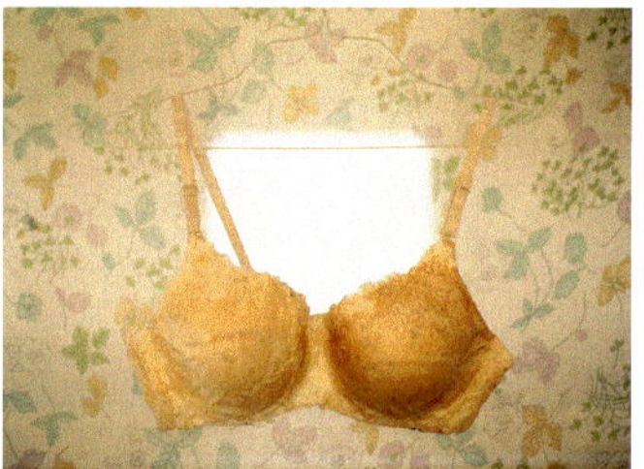
Waxed Bra
Bridgehampton, 2003

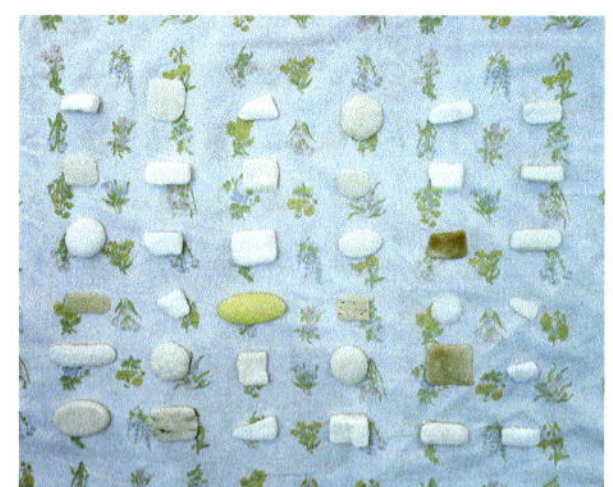
Collection of Soaps
Bridgehampton, 2003

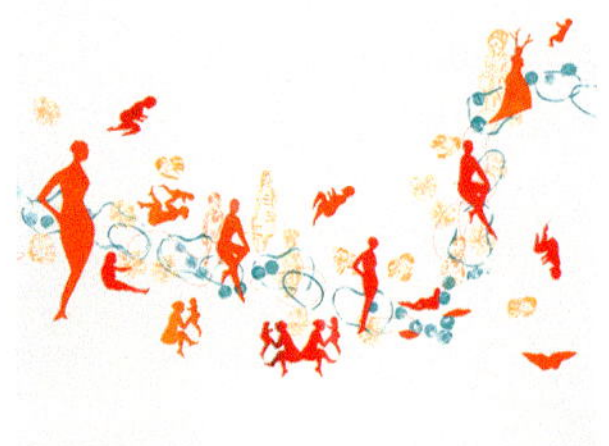
Orange Pastoral of Women (Detail)
Mixed Media on Paper, 48 x 90 inches,
2009

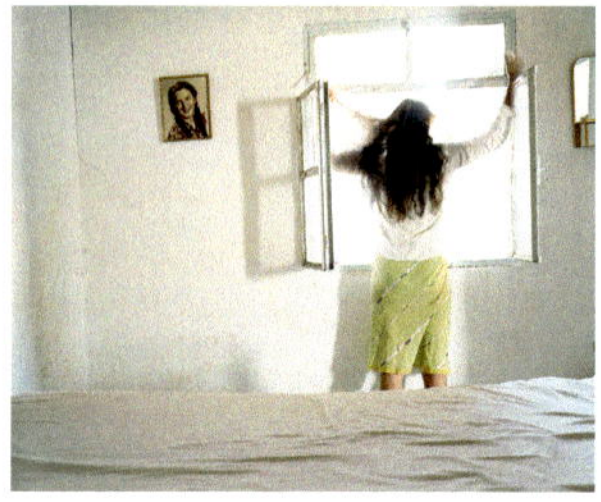
Looking out of the Window
Samos, Greece, 2004

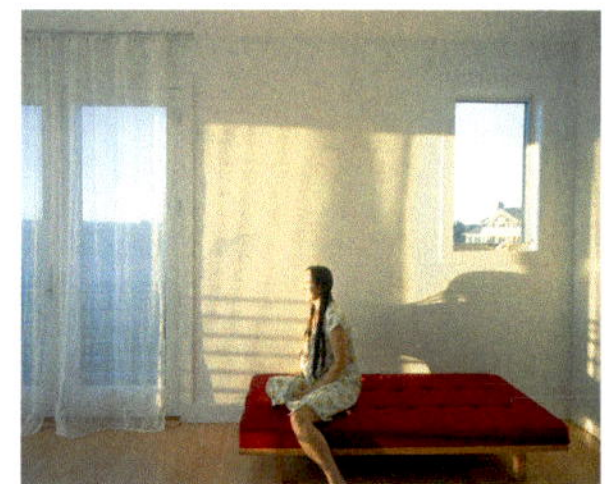
The Red Daybed
Bridgehampton, 2004

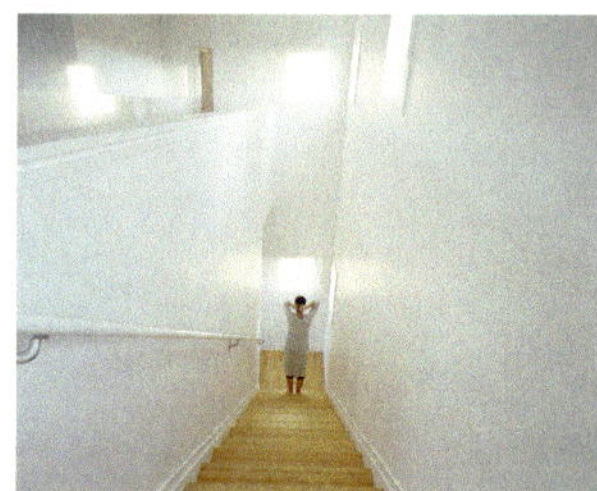
Descending Staircase
Bridgehampton, 2004

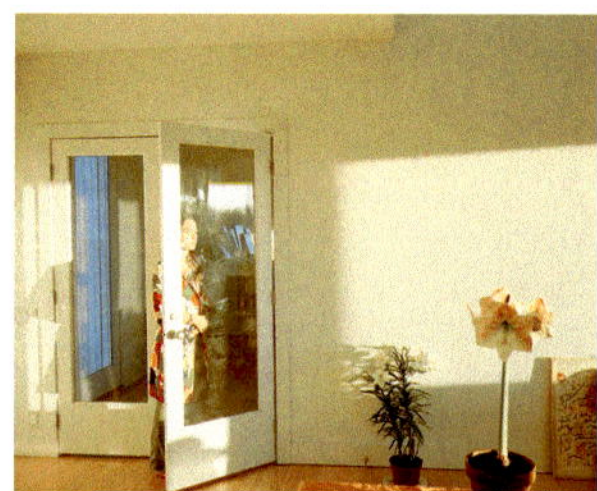
Hokusai's Dream
Bridgehampton, 2005

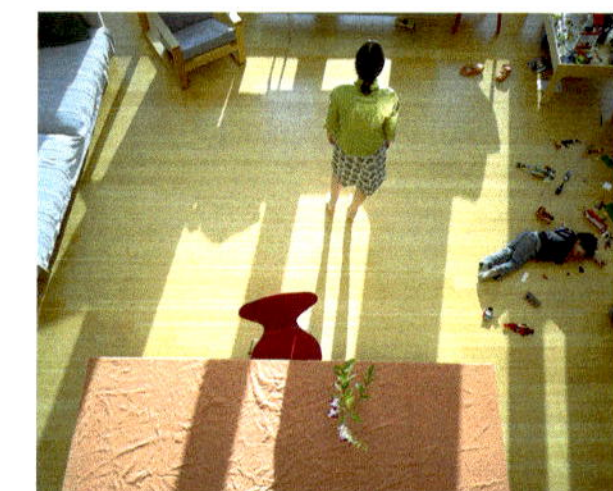
Julian and his Lego
Bridgehampton, 2005

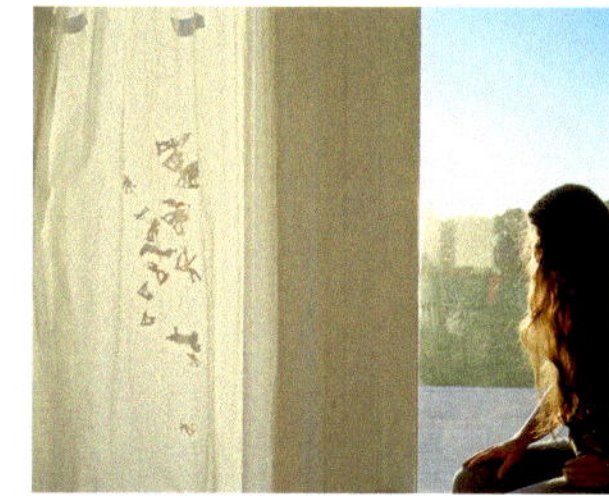
Toy Soldiers and Silhouette
Bridgehampton, 2004

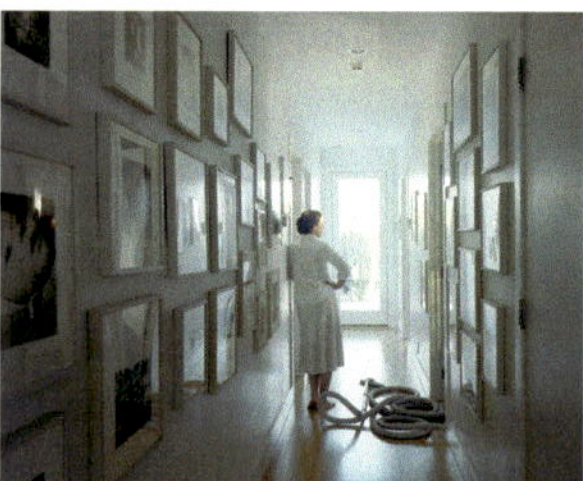
Vacuum Cleaner
Bridgehampton, 2006

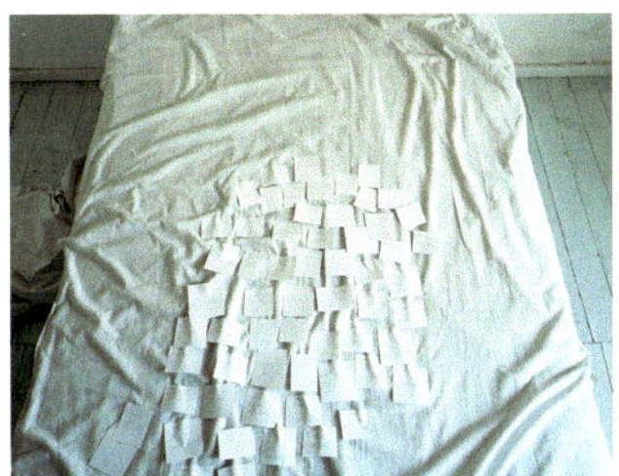
Notes on Bed
Samos, Greece, 2006

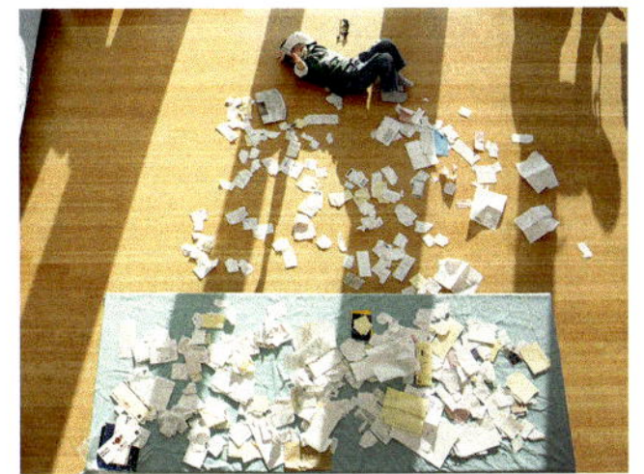
Tax Time
Bridgehampton, 2006

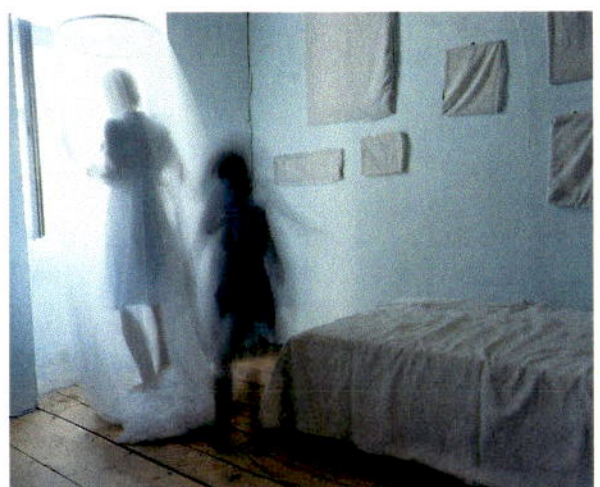
Turquoise Room and Wrapped Photographs
Samos, 2008

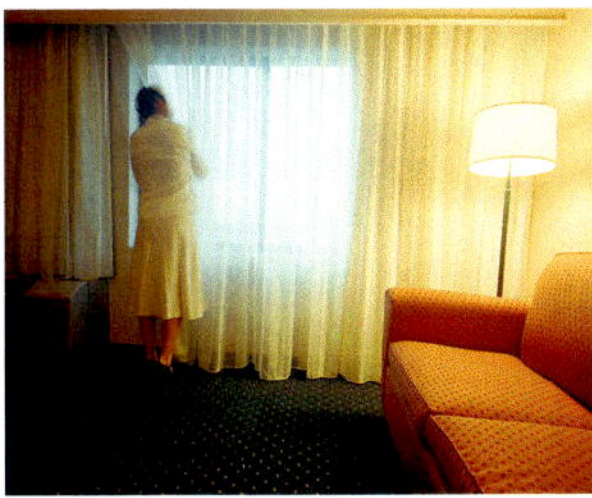
Hotel Room
Amarillo, 2006

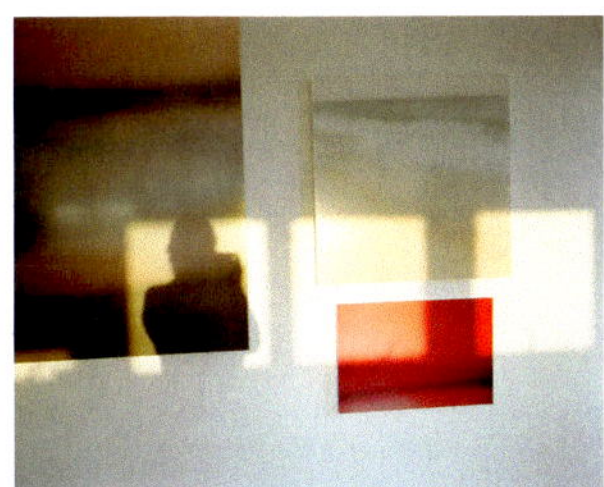
Philippe's Photographs
Bridgehampton, 2009

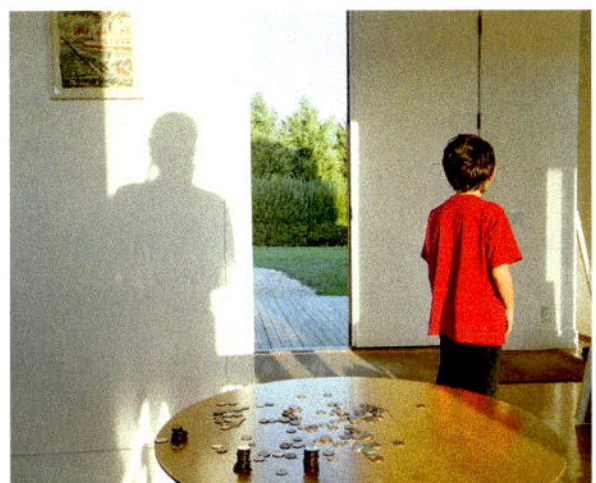
The Money Counter
Bridgehampton, 2009

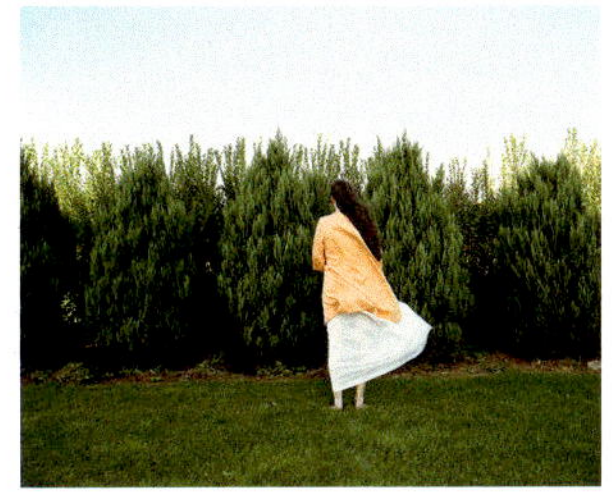
Morning Breeze
Bridgehampton, 2004

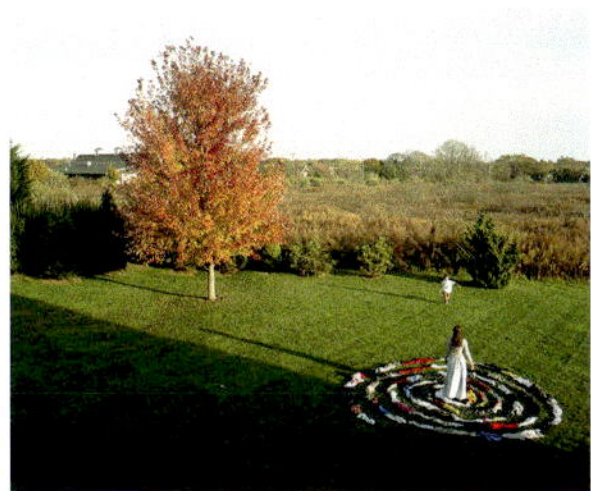
The Laundry Spiral
Bridgehampton, 2009

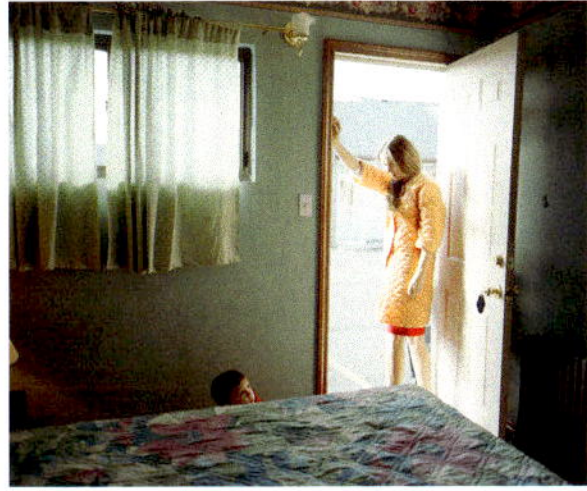
Hotel Room
Patchogue, 2004

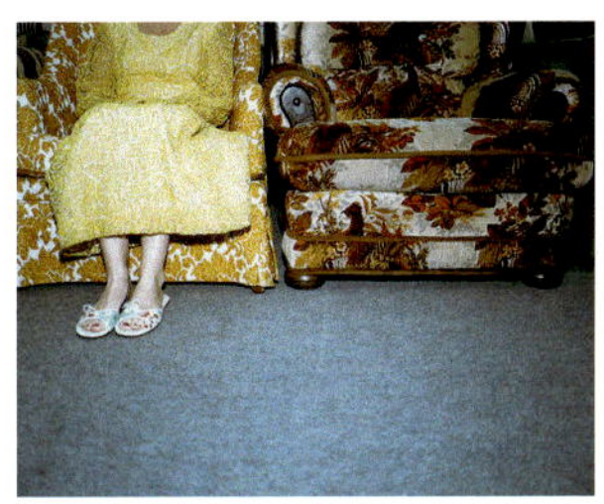
The Yellow Dress
Patchogue, 2004

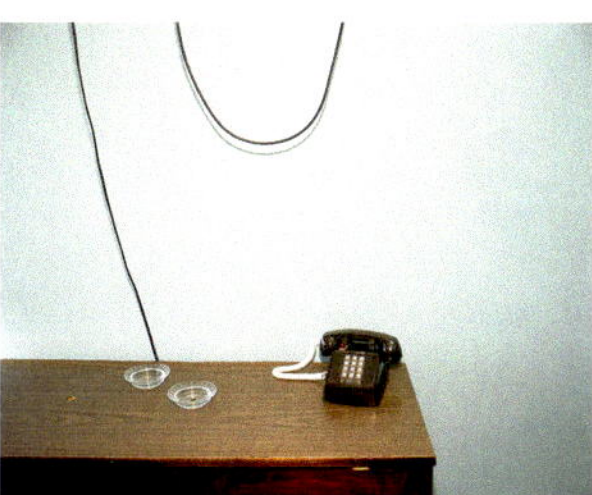
Telephone
Patchogue, 2004

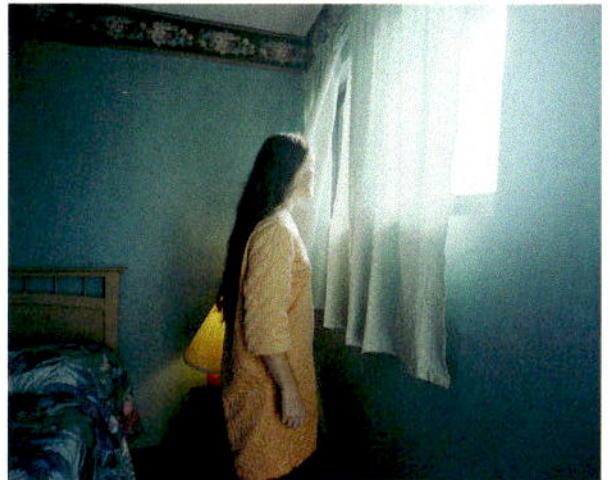
Room with no View
Patchogue, 2004

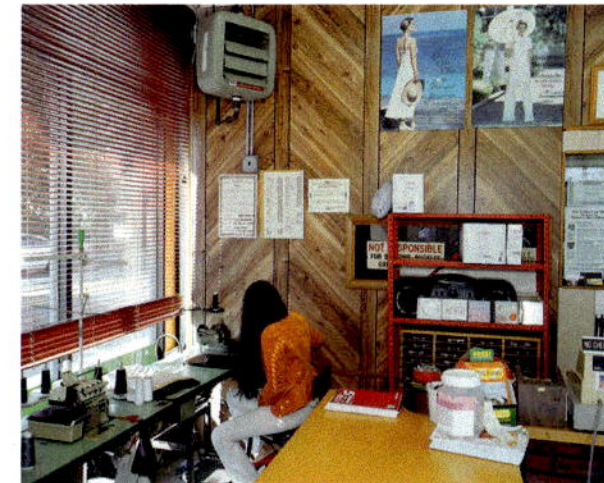
The Dry Cleaner
Sayville, 2005

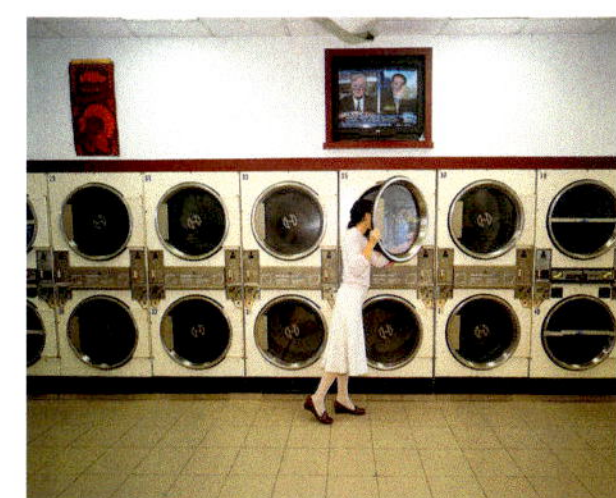
Laundromat
Patchogue, 2004

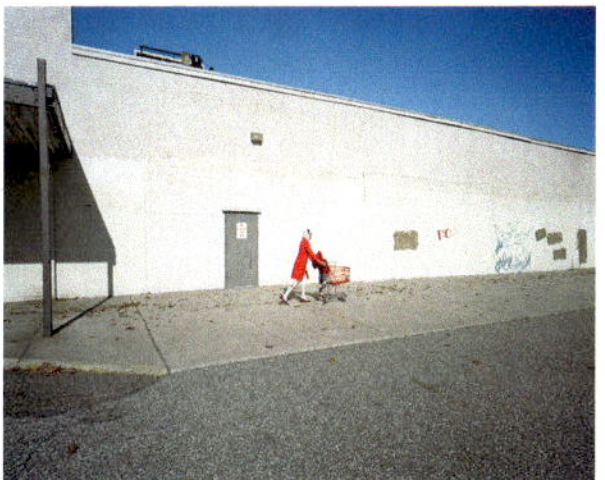
Shopping Mall
Sayville, 2005

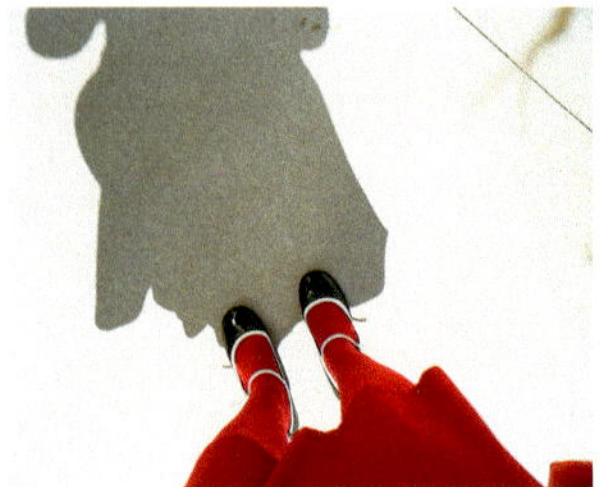
Swearing-in Ceremony as an American Citizen
Islip, 2009

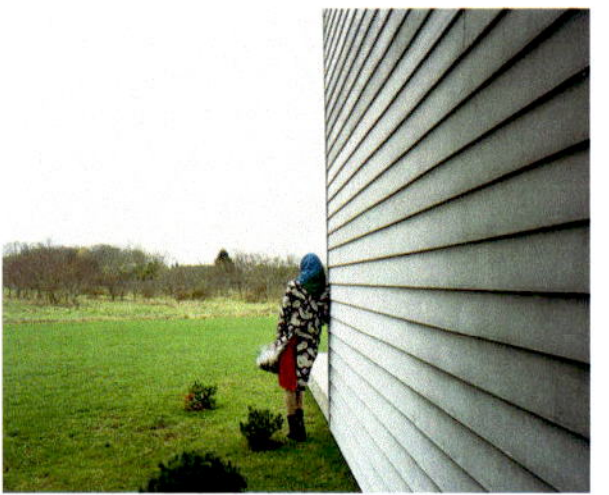
Gray House Wall
Bridgehampton, 2003

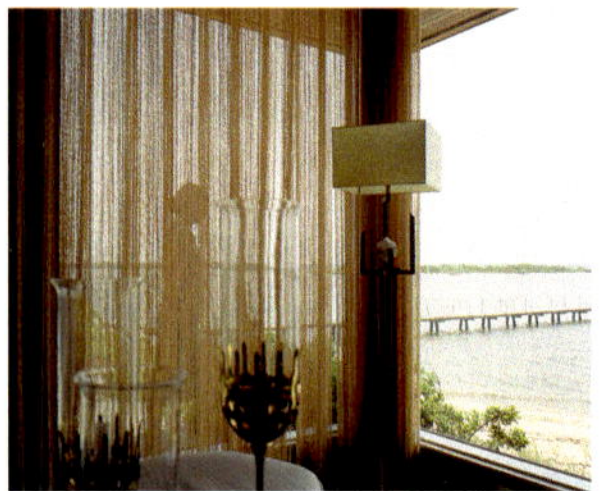
Curtain
Shelter Island, 2005

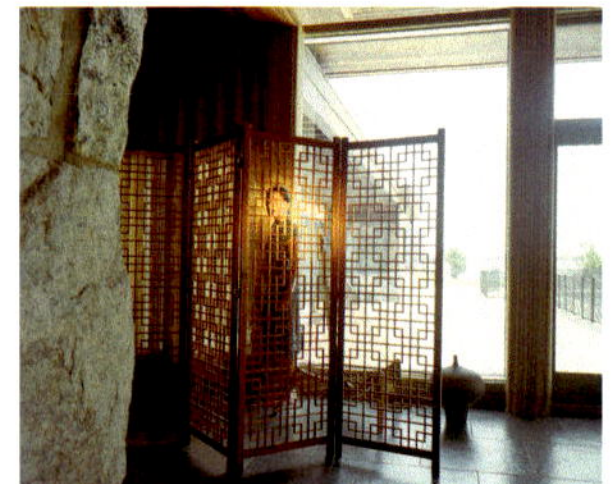
The Paravent
Shelter Island, 2005

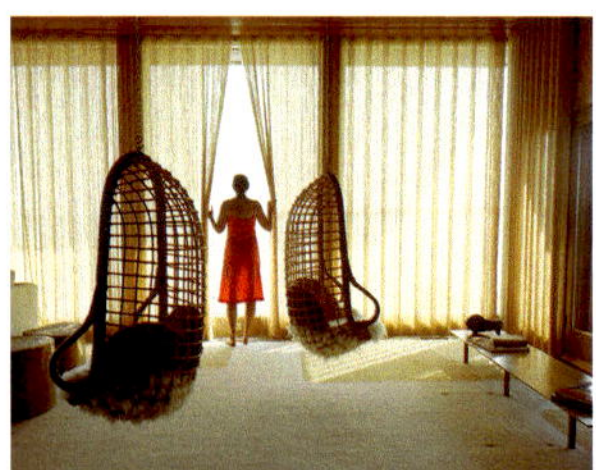
Hanging Chairs
Shelter Island, 2005

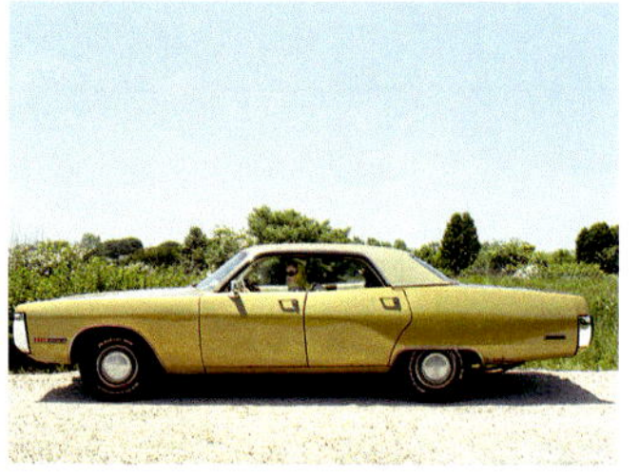
Yellow Car
Bridgehampton, 2005

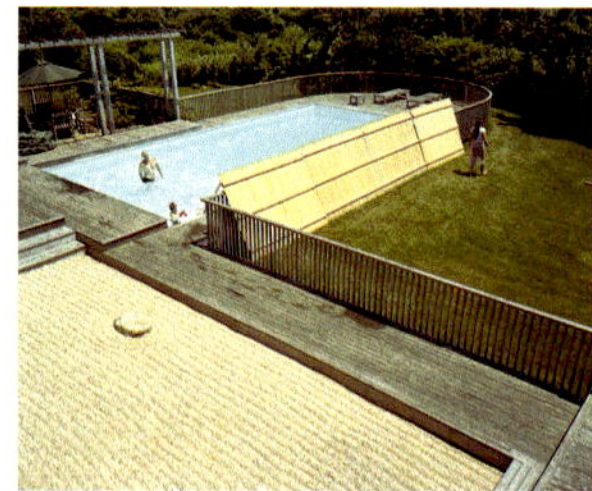
Pool
Sagaponack, 2005

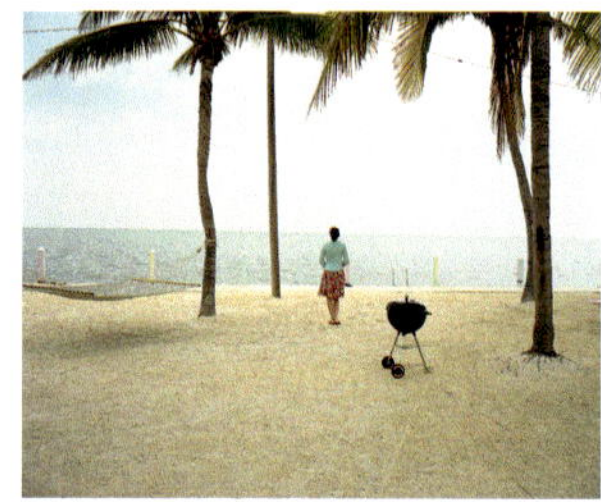
Barbeque
Key West, 2006

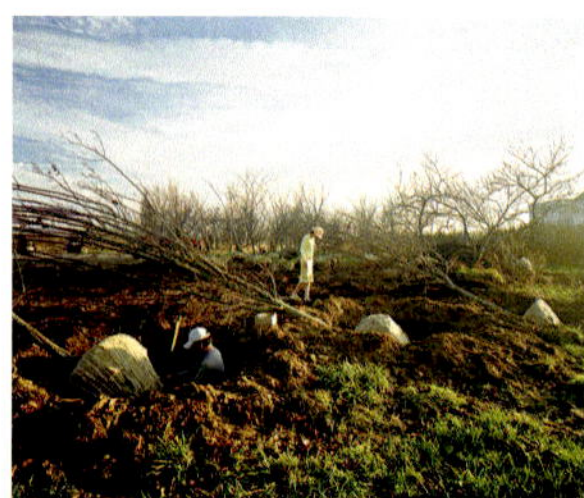
Tree Farm
Bridgehampton, 2004

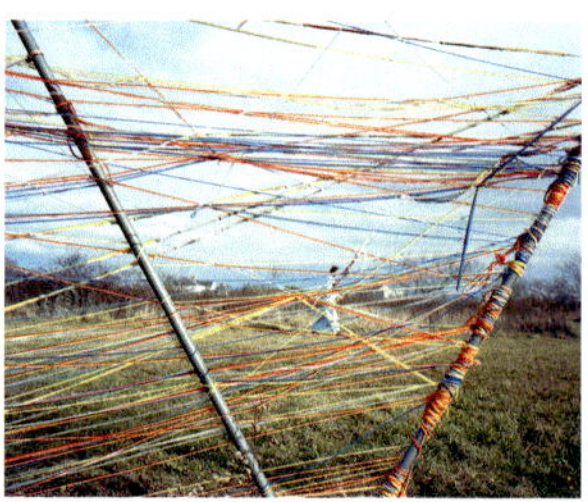
Strings Attached
Bridgehampton, 2009

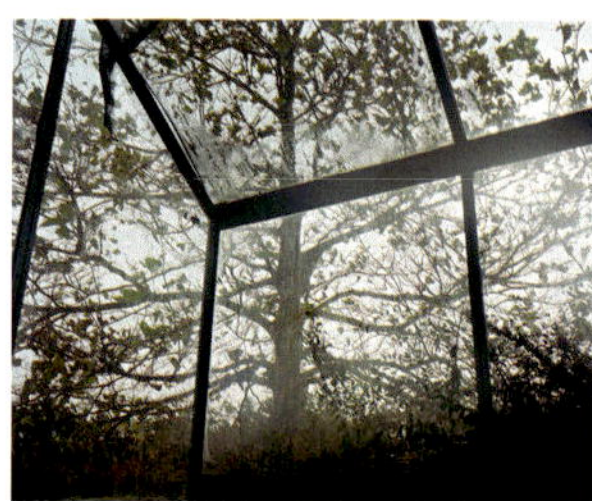
Greenhouse
Sagaponack, 2005

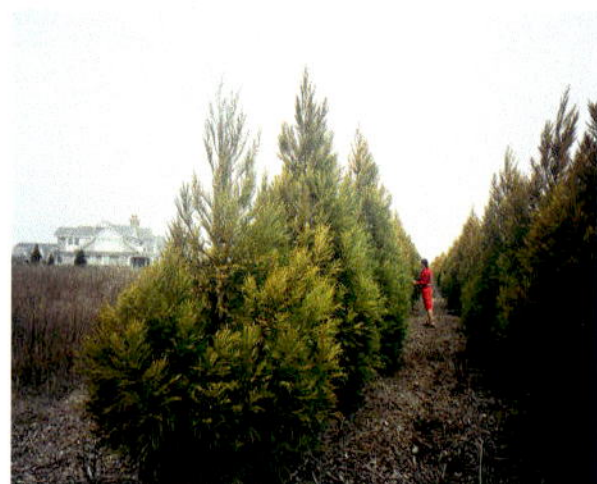
Spec House for Sale
Bridgehampton, 2007

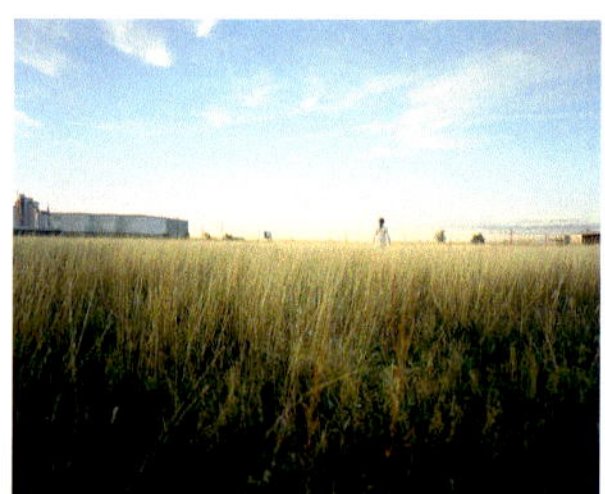
Movie Theater in a Field
Amarillo, 2004

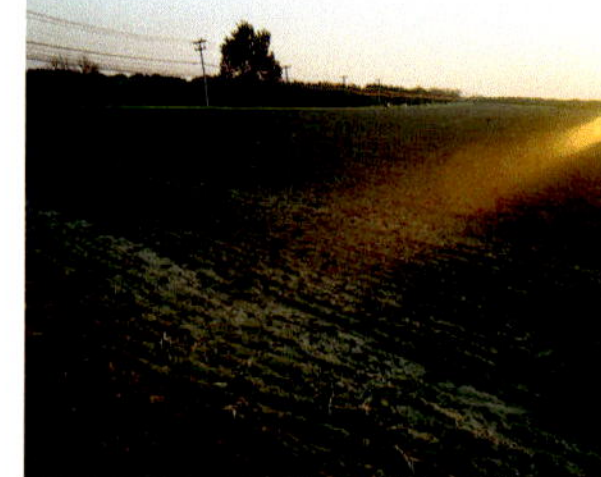
Sunset on Scuttlehole Road
Bridgehampton, 2009

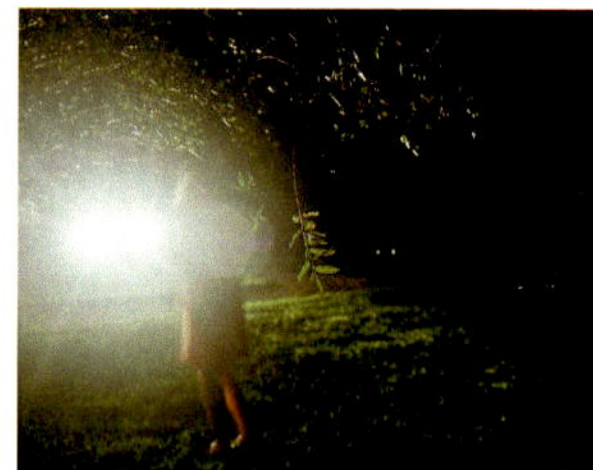
Car Lights
Bridgehampton, 2009

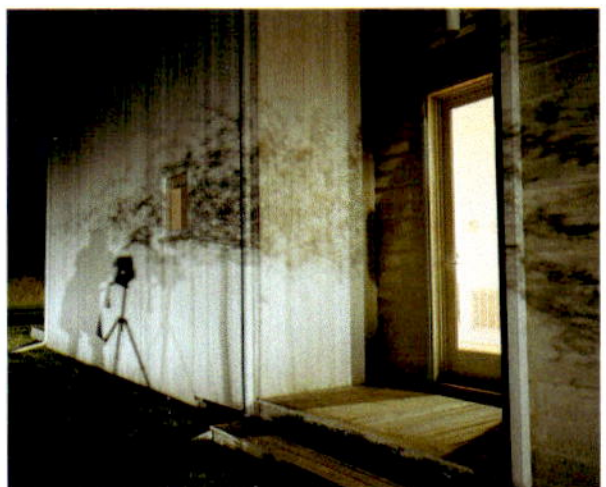
The Camera and the Nishiki Tree
Bridgehampton, 2009

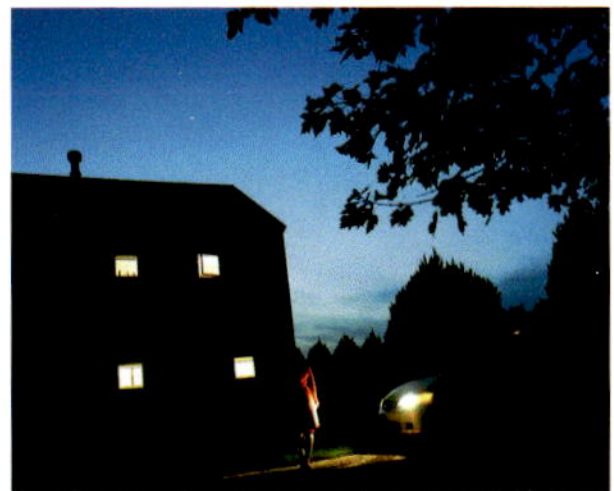
House
Bridgehampton, 2009

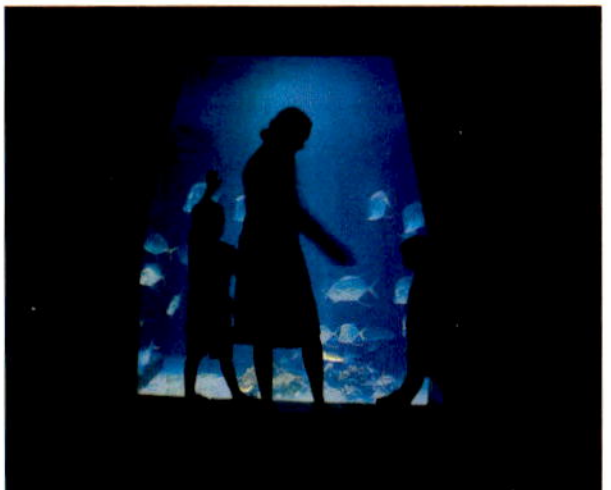
Aquarium
Paradise Island, 2005

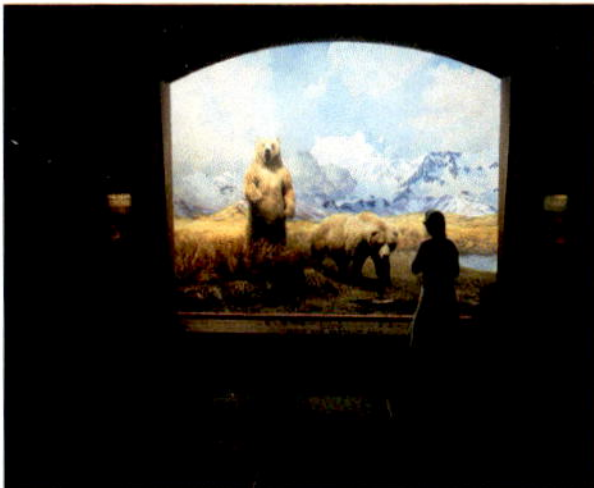
Bear at the Museum of Natural History
New York, 2004

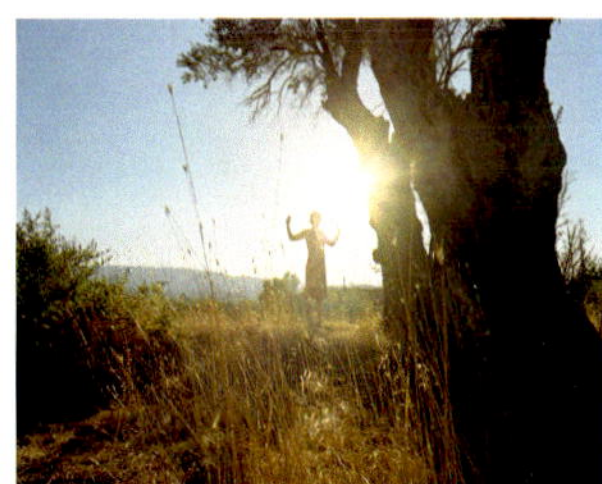
Strong Woman and Olive Tree
Samos, Greece, 2004

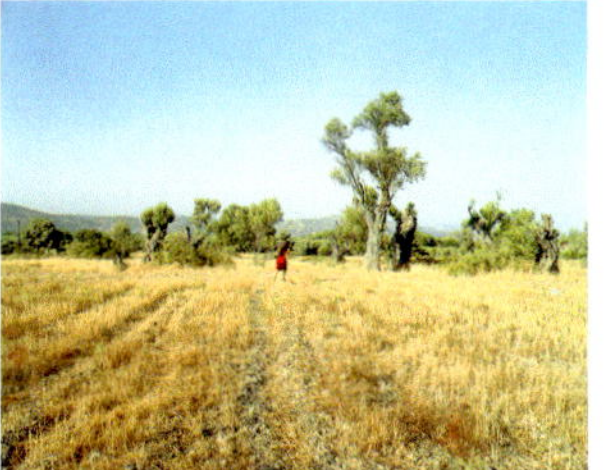
Running in Red Skirt
Samos, Greece, 2004

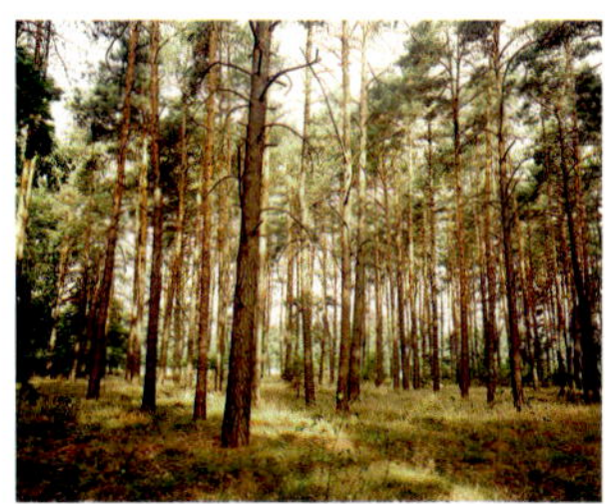
The Woods
Strehlen, Germany, 2003

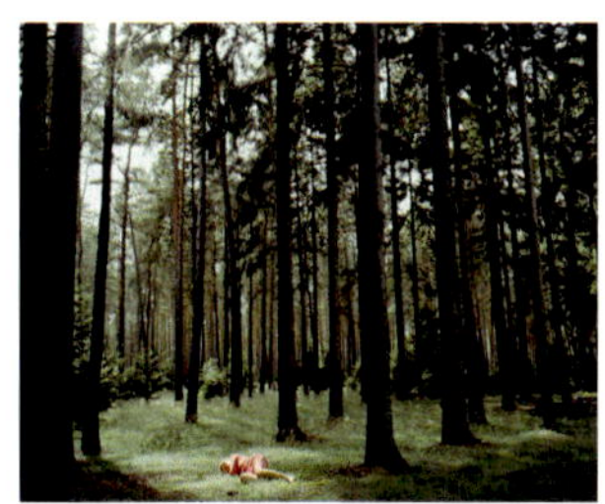
Sleeping in the Woods
Strehlen, Germany, 2004

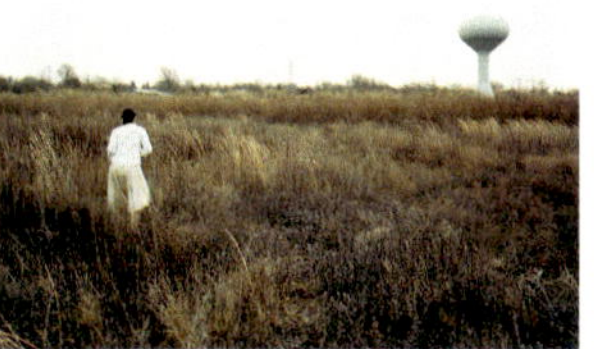
Woman in Field with Water Tower
Southampton, 2007

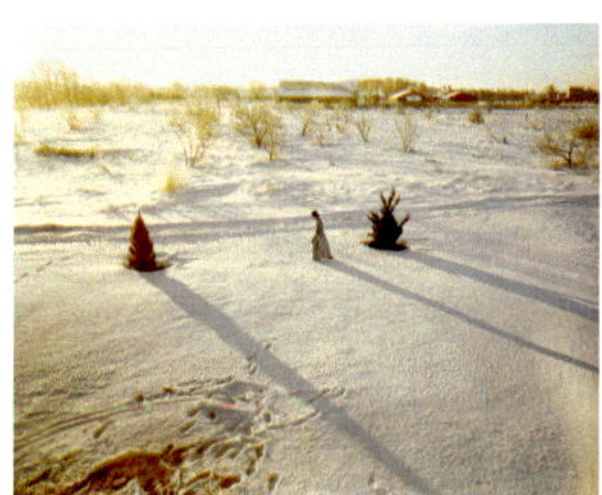
Walk in Snow
Bridgehampton, 2005

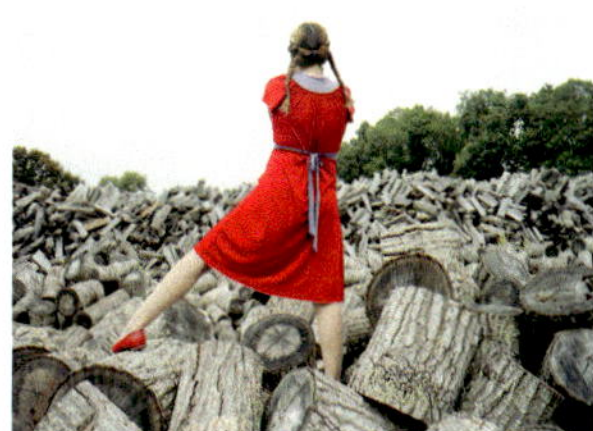
The Red Dress
Sagaponack, 2008

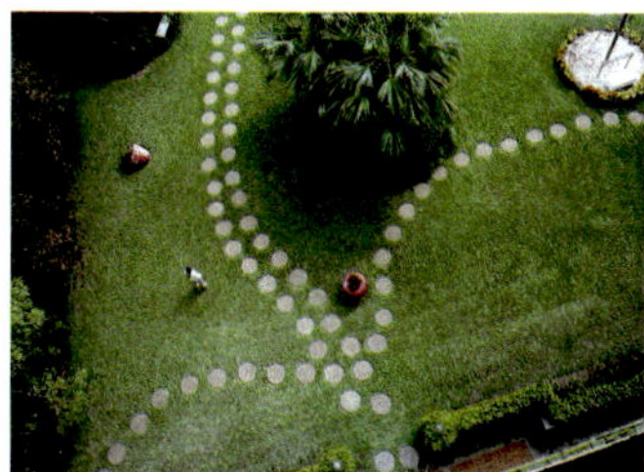
Lawn in Coconut Grove
Florida, 2005

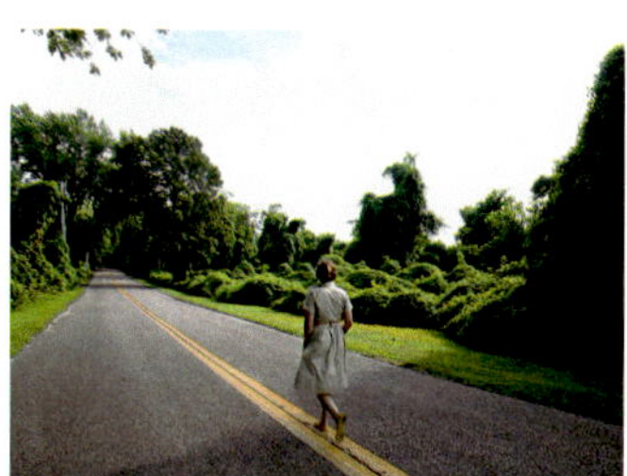
The Walk
Shelter Island, 2008

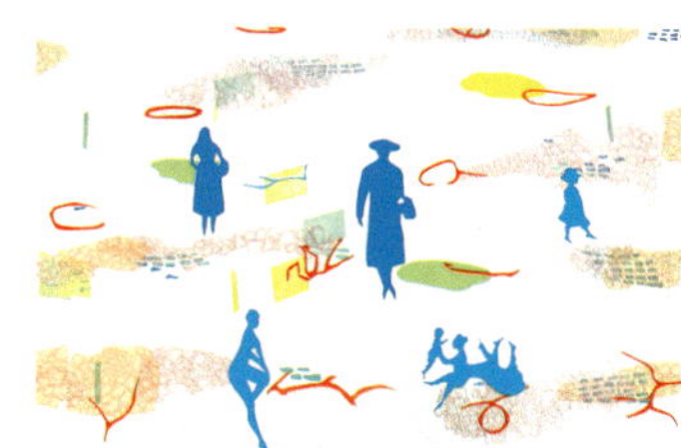
Blue Silhouettes and Topography (Detail)
Mixed Media on Paper, 48 x 90 inches,
2008

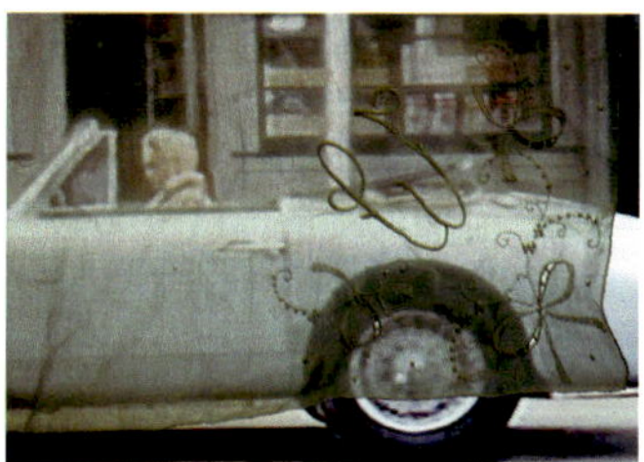
Car and Monogrammed Handkerchief
Film Still, 2007

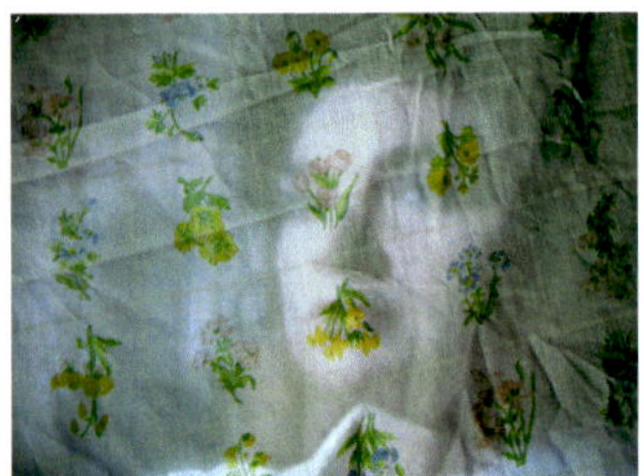
Face behind Flower Curtain
Film Still, 2008

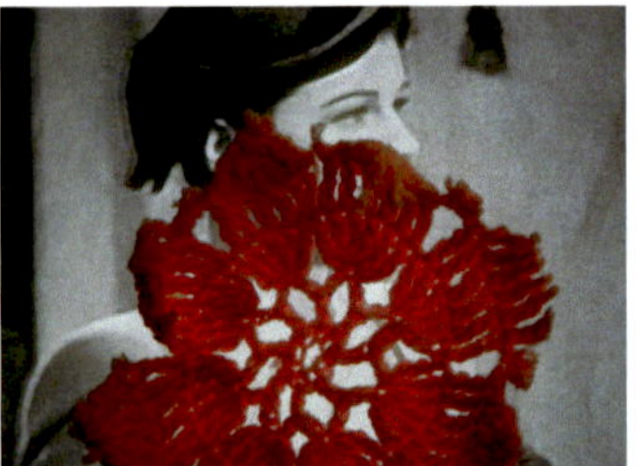
Woman and Pink Doily
Film Still, 2007

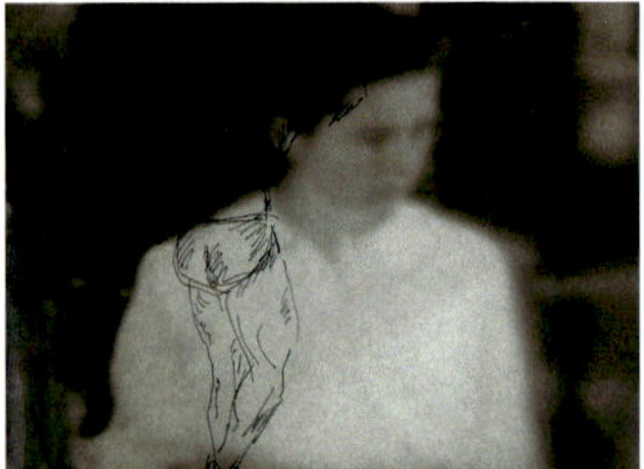
Girl and Drawing of a Strong Man
Film Still, 2008

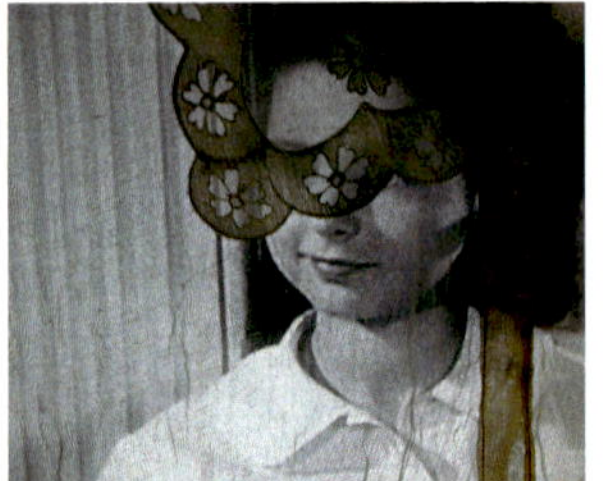
Girl and Doily
Film Still, 2007

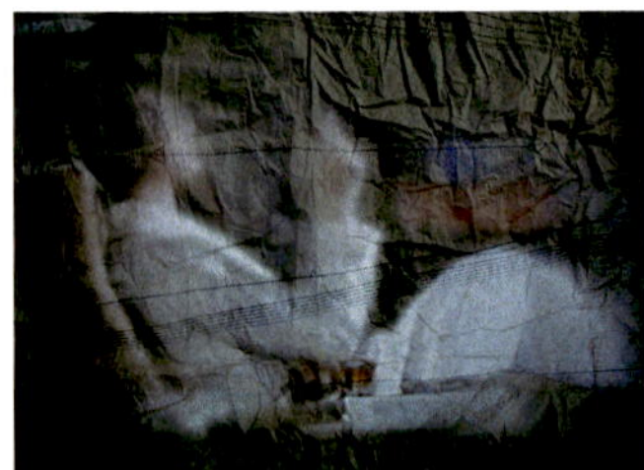
Sewing Pattern
Film Still, 2007

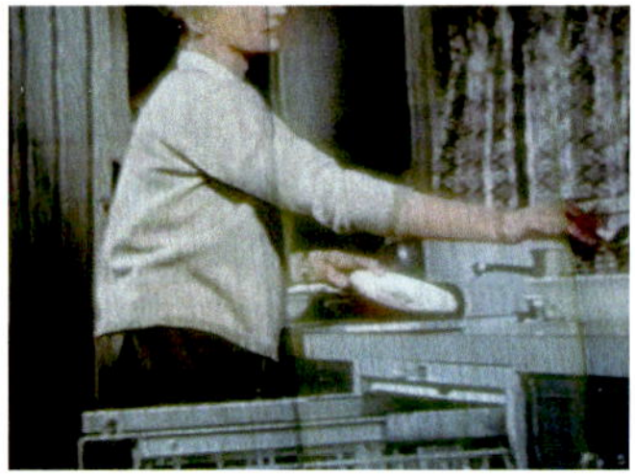
The Dishwasher
Film Still, 2007

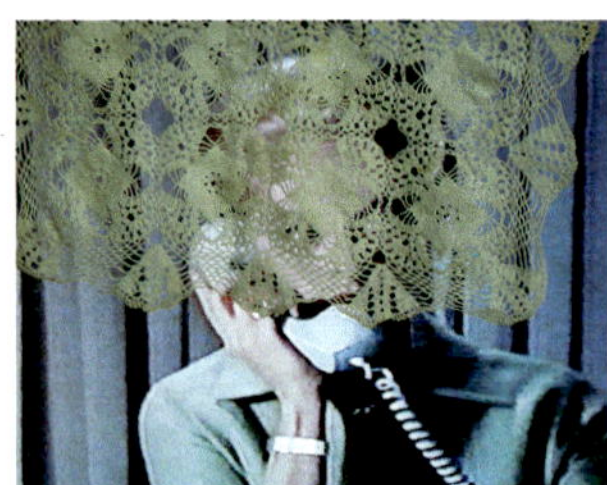
The Telephone Call
Film Still, 2007

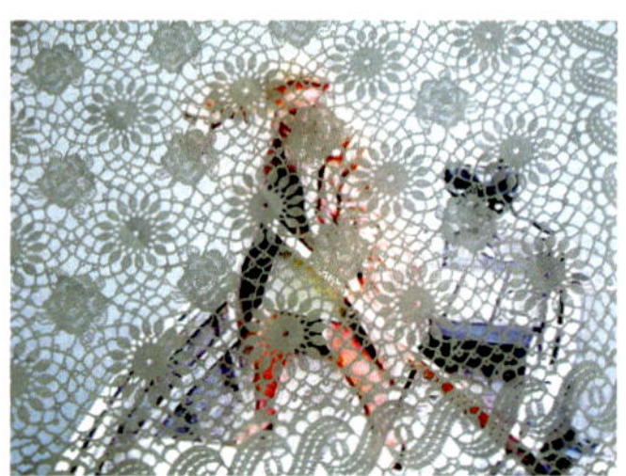
The Wobbly Boat
Film Still, 2007

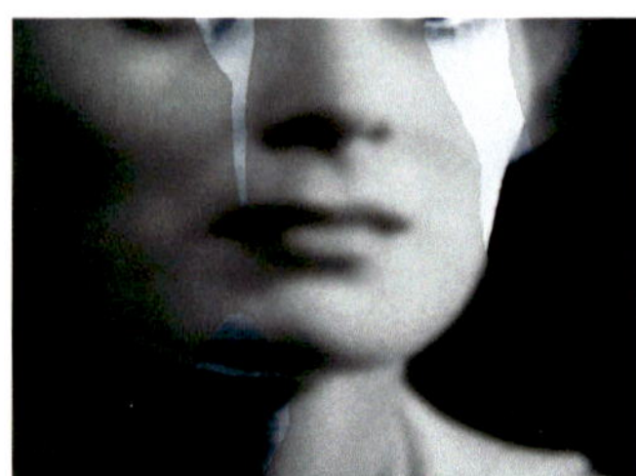
Face with Ripped Paper
Film Still, 2007

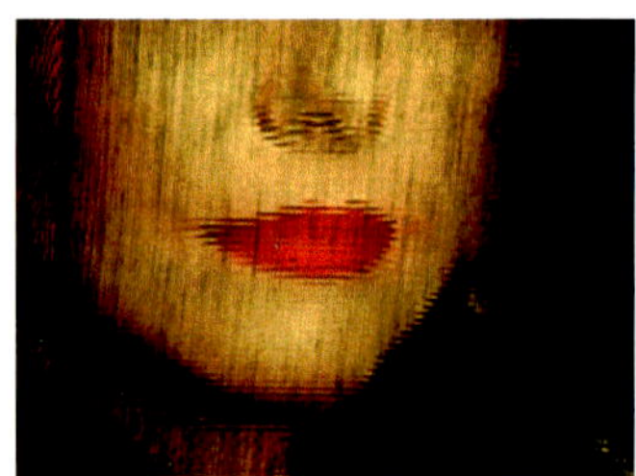
Yellow Fabric and Red Mouth
Film Still, 2007

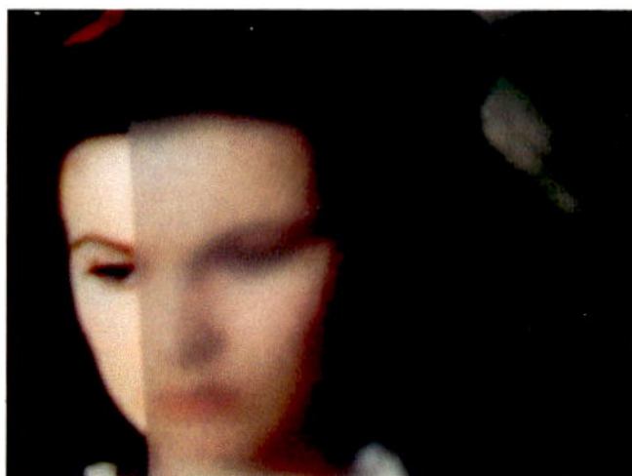
Woman with Red Hairband
Film Still, 2007

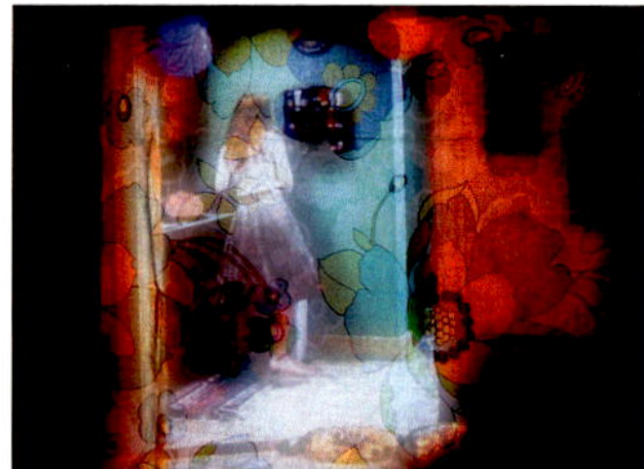
The Kitchen and Flower Curtain
Film Still, 2006

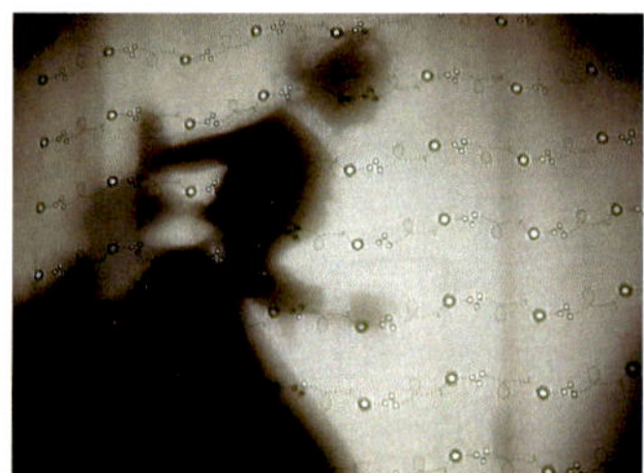
Running Woman
Film Still, 2007

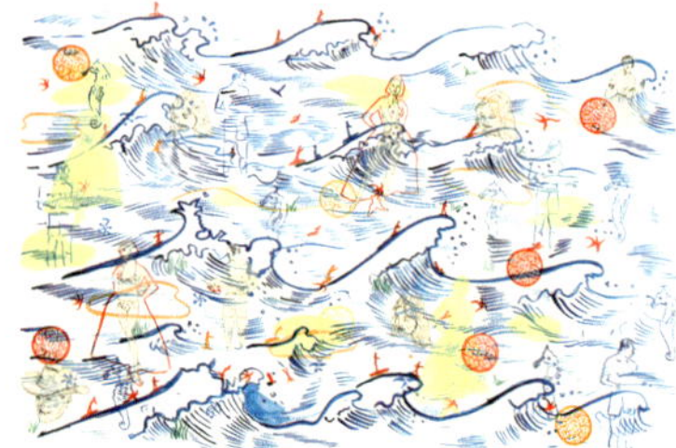
Women and the WaveMixed Media on Paper,
30 x 44 inches, 2007

THANKS

Bastienne Schmidt is a German born and New York based fine art photographer and multi media artist. She has lived and worked for many years in Greece and Italy.
Her art work is included in the collections of the Museum of Modern Art in New York, the International Center of Photography, The Brooklyn Museum, The Victoria and Albert Museum in London, the Bibliotheque Nationale in Paris among many others. She has previously published *Vivir la Muerte, American Dreams* and *ShadowHome. Home Stills* is her fourth book.

Many thanks to Jochen Visscher for understanding the underlying vision of *Home Stills*, to Vicki Goldberg for her thoughtful and insightful text, and to Susanne Rösler and Philipp Sperrle from jovis for their input into the editorial and technical aspects of producing this book.
I would like to thank Kevin Miller and the Southeast Museum of Photography for showing *Home Stills* and also to Juliana Romnes for taking care of all the practical details involved.

Many thanks to Liz and Kirk Radke, for your friendship, your loyalty and continued artistic support; to Ed Osowski for being a long time supporter and believer in my projects; to Toni Ross for your friendship and for exploring different artistic and cultural turfs together, might it be in Egypt, Paris, or New York; to Anita Naughton for your insights, laughter and years of friendship.
And thanks to all of you for an open and ongoing dialogue as friends and art connoisseurs: Glynis Berry, Carolin Bohlmann, Peter Hammel, Julia Herzberg, Susan Kismaric, Alicia Longwell, Jordan Mejias, Evan Mirapaul, Elena Prohaska, Andrea Stern, Christina Mossaides Strassfield, Christoph Tannert.
I thank my friends here on the East End and the Hayground community and those afar, for all your support over the years. And to Britta, for being the Mary Poppins to our children; it was fun to roam together!
And thanks to my family for fostering an atmosphere of creativity and freedom, my mother Uta and my siblings Pascale, Florian, Benjamin, Sophie and their families.
I love you Max, Julian and Philippe! Thanks for accompanying me on the adventurous forays into these unknown countries of domestic spaces.

Cover: *The Red Dress*, 2008

Concept: Bastienne Schmidt
Design: Bastienne Schmidt, Susanne Rösler
Lithography: Bild1Druck, Berlin
Printing and binding: Grafisches Centrum Cuno, Calbe

Bibliographic information published by the Deutsche Nationalbibliothek
The Deutsche Nationalbibliothek lists this publication in the Deutsche Nationalbibliografie; detailed bibliographic data are available on the Internet at http://dnb.d-nb.de

jovis Verlag GmbH
Kurfürstenstraße 15/16
10785 Berlin

www.jovis.de

ISBN 978-3-86859-069-2

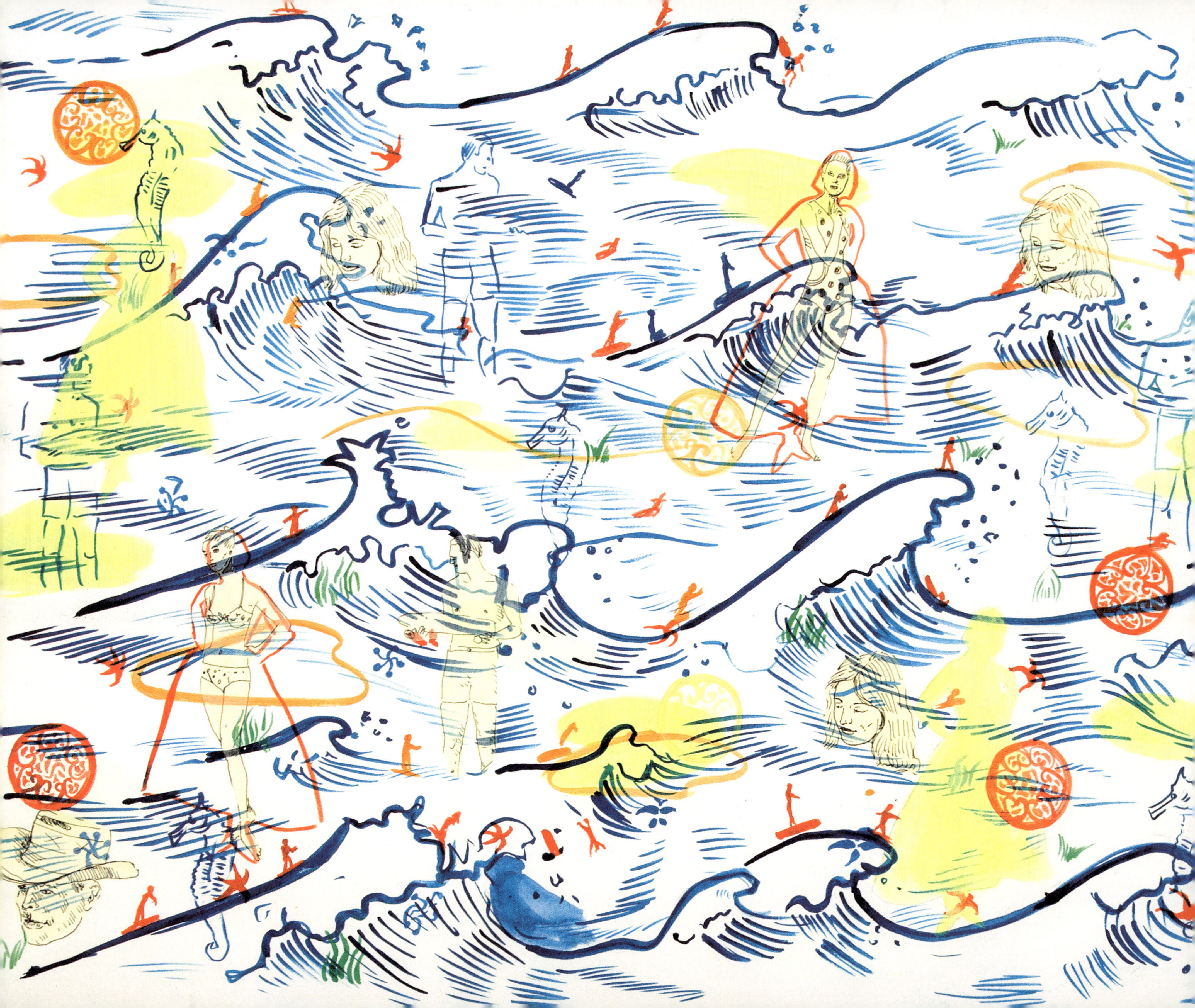